BIRMINGHAM BUILDINGS

BIRMINGHAM BUILDINGS

The Architectural Story of a
Midland City

BRYAN LITTLE

David & Charles : Newton Abbot

ISBN 0 7153 5295 4

Set in 10 on 12 pt Plantin
by Bristol Typesetting Company Limited
and printed in Great Britain
by Redwood Press Limited
for David & Charles (Publishers) Limited
South Devon House Newton Abbot Devon

CONTENTS

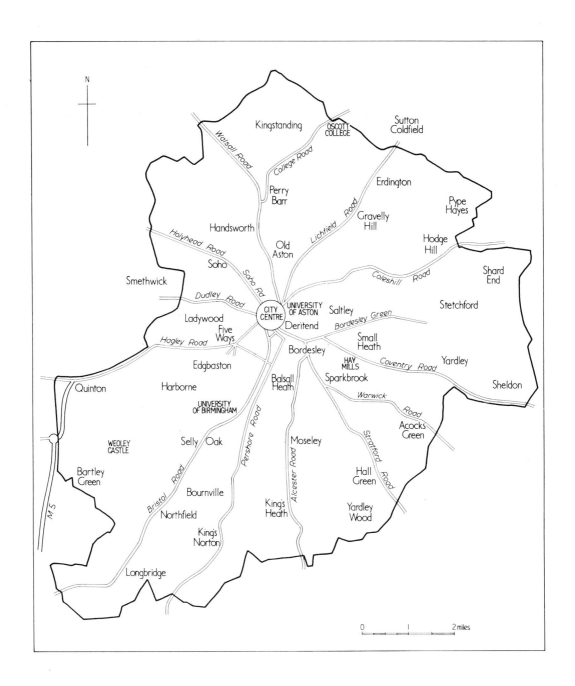

The Architectural Story

MEDIEVAL BEGINNINGS

Late in the reign of Henry VIII, when the antiquarian traveller John Leland came to Birmingham, he found a town of 'black and white' half-timbered houses which we should now consider attractive and picturesque. From Deritend on the bank of the little River Rea which lay in the larger parish of Aston, up through Digbeth and on past Birmingham's parish church of St Martin, the street rose, as it still rises, to the main business centre of the small market town which had grown up in this tract of countryside near the meeting point of Warwickshire, Staffordshire, and Worcestershire. It was in this one street that Leland found the main 'beauty' of this 'good market town' whose inhabitants, clothmaking and commerce apart, were already much committed to the metal trades. They drew ready supplies of iron and coal from nearby Staffordshire, gaining increasing skill so that knives, cutting tools, bits and nails were all made by the smiths, lorimers and nailers whose forges and workshops stood, as became traditional in Birmingham, in back yards and gardens.

What Leland saw was a place where timber-framed houses, and the few which were built of the local sandstone, shared in the building tradition of the west Midlands—a region which was well wooded but not specially rich in building stone. Some houses, like the Old Crown on Deritend High Street and the Golden Lion which has, for some sixty years, stood on its new site in Cannon Hill Park, were aligned to the streets; others, with their narrower, gabled frontages, ran back from the roads. In both cases they displayed a varied, increasingly complex pattern of dark timber and a lightly coloured plaster infilling. Panelling, in late Gothic architectural patterns, could have appeared on bargeboards and on some other timbers, while the Old Crown suggests that by the early Tudor years brick, more durably fireproof than local sandstone, was used for chimney stacks. Only in St Martin's church, perhaps in the moated manor house, and in the buildings of the priory which was really a hospital or almshouse run by religious brethren, was stone used as a main material. St Martin's was Birmingham's chief medieval building, completed soon before or shortly after 1300. Its sturdy north-western tower had simple chamfered arches, without capitals to their jambs, leading through from the tower space to the nave and its southern aisle. Its arcades and windows were of the early Decorated period. The spire, as in many Midland churches, gave it conspicuous distinction; this same graceful feature of a stone spire rose high at Aston, King's Norton and Yardley.

These more distant churches have also to be considered in a book whose subject is the architecture of the whole area within Birmingham's current boundaries. So too one must reckon with some houses and with the towered churches at Sheldon and Edgbaston which were in Warwickshire, at Harborne and Handsworth which lay in Staffordshire, and at Northfield which belonged to Worcestershire. These villages, in

7

those early days, had few nks with the town which was later to absorb them; only the medieval chapel and some houses at Deritend, in the great parish of Aston yet not (except in times of flood) very noticeably parted from Birmingham by the rustling Rea, were in the same urban concentration as the somewhat larger town. Not till this century were these portions of the three adjoining counties taken into the great city whose rise had come from the metal-working industry. Many buildings of importance for present-day Birmingham's architectural story were not, when built, within the town. As in St Martin's parish, the oldest of them shared in the timber or sandstone building techniques of the west Midlands. From the blocked late Norman window in the tower at Handsworth, through the somewhat later Norman doorway and the thirteenth-century splendour of the chancel at Northfield, to the good later Gothic work in the churches at Sheldon, Aston, King's Norton and Yardley, and to the humble late medieval towers at Edgbaston, Moseley and Harborne, the sum total of Birmingham's medieval church architecture is considerable. Nor should one overlook half-timbered secular buildings; at Yardley and King's Norton they are as good as the amazing survival of the Old Crown at Deritend.

ELIZABETHAN AND STUART

Under Elizabeth I and the early Stuarts, Birmingham's building work was confined to houses, with a little more variety than before in the materials chosen and with the one great mansion, Aston Hall, whose size and style put it among the more important buildings of its time.

Most new houses in Birmingham and in the parishes near a town whose houses, by the 1670s, exceeded in number those of Stratford on Avon and Sutton Coldfield elsewhere in Warwickshire, were still half-timbered. The Golden Lion in Deritend may have been of this Elizabethan period, and not a survival from before Leland's time. More certainly late Elizabethan or Jacobean are Blakesley Hall out at Yardley and, much closer to the modern city's centre, the attractive Stratford House at Bordesley. The square-headed entrance to its porch, and the complex curvature of the timber pattern in its gables, place it soon before or shortly after the year 1600. More notable, out at Tile Cross and near the eastern edge of modern Birmingham, is the central, oldest section of the unassuming but attractive manor house of Sheldon Hall. It is mainly of red and dark blue brick, but with stone dressings and an array of square-headed, mullioned windows both in the original house and in its somewhat later wings which were added, in the accepted fashion of such 'manorial' houses, at right angles to the line of the hall block. The gables all have the triangular silhouette normal at their particular dates. More entertaining, and resembling the patterns common in the Netherlands, was the outline of the main gables of the house at Cooper's Mills, perhaps of brick and almost certainly of the seventeenth century, which Westley's eastern view of Birmingham, dated 1731 and one of two which well picture the early Georgian town, shows down towards the Rea. It lay north-east of the highway through Deritend whose small medieval chapel still stood when Westley recorded it. Far more important, out to the north, was the great country mansion completed about 1635.

The Holte family had long been at Aston before Sir Thomas, a man of wealth and a baronet since 1612, decided to build, on an empty site not far from the parish church, a mansion of such size and splendour as almost to rank with the great 'prodigy houses' of the Elizabethans. He started in 1618, and though he occupied the house in 1631 it was incomplete till 1635. Though Inigo Jones had by now designed several buildings for court patrons in the fully classical Palladian style, Aston Hall, with its essentially 'manorial' though symmetrical plan, and with Gothic references in the plain mullions of its windows, belongs to the more gropingly Renaissance phase of English architecture. Within that grouping it is important, and is a great glory of modern Birmingham.

Ground plans of Aston Hall, showing some variations from its actual arrangement, appear in John Thorpe's collection of architectural plans. It is just possible that Thorpe had a hand in the designing of Sir Thomas Holte's new house. The most striking element in the hall's planning is its symmetry, best seen in the great forecourt which faces east towards the church and Castle Bromwich. Delightful little gabled and mullioned pavilion lodges lead up to the mansion whose wings, with their bow windows, Flemish-type gables and courtyard towers, exactly balance each other. The central block's main frontage juts out a little, with a bold array of transomed windows to light the hall, and with a main doorway in Jacobean-cum-baroque taste, whose upper stage contains the Holte arms and an inscription recording the mansion's building process. The hall, symmetrically arranged on each side of its main doorways, is a genuine entrance hall and a deviation from the plans drawn by Thorpe. Its panelling, landscapes and frieze of plaster animals, make it an attractive introduction to the splendours of the interior.

The other exterior fronts of Aston Hall have to be seen before one studies the rest of what lies inside. The southern front, with more gables in the Dutch or Flemish manner, is the most attractive, with arched loggias and shell-headed niches flanking the central projection which once contained the chapel, more recently used as a dining room. That projection was at first more seemly than it is now, for Thorpe's plan, and more recent excavations, have proved that a star-shaped projection once jutted fancifully from the centre. Projecting windows, one a half octagon and the other two rectangular, also added interest to the garden front whose lower windows light reception rooms while the upper windows, large and doubly transomed, admit ample light to the long gallery which was still, for Jacobean landlords, a fancied feature of their more lavish homes. The altered northern front masks the kitchen and domestic offices.

The lavish early Stuart character of Aston Hall's interior best appears in the great drawing room, the main staircase, the pilasters and the plaster ceiling of the long gallery, and in the strapwork plaster ceiling and animal frieze (recalling that in the entrance hall) in the bedroom known as King Charles' Room. The great staircase, with its lavishly pierced banister panels and heavy, over-ornate newel posts crowned by herm-like finials with pendents below them, is of a barbaric splendour less pleasing than the best features of the Summer Parlour, or Great Drawing Room, which is the house's most attractive room. Here the fireplace is again in the Flemish Renaissance taste, but with a more graceful touch than one finds in the staircase. The strapwork of the ceiling is richly scrolled, and in the equally rich frieze the eleven niches contain classically armed figures of the Nine Worthies and two additional heroes.

Despite the town's steady growth, the late seventeenth century seems to have been of little note in Birmingham's architectural history. No houses of this period survive, but some with horizontal, corniced fronts may well have been built, along with others in the gable-fronted tradition which had earlier prevailed. In the 1690s the weathered stonework of the nave and chancel of St Martin's was encased, for better protection, in the now widely accepted material of brick, with round-headed Renaissance windows replacing the pointed and traceried ones of some four centuries before. Nonconformist chapels were openly built once William and Mary were in power; the Old Meeting, of about 1690, had four gables, two pedimented doorways, and square-headed windows in a domestic looking façade. More interesting, a few years earlier, had been the short-lived effort to give a worthy worshipping place to the town's Catholic congregation.

A chapel, in what became known as Mass House Lane, was started in 1687 and finished next year. Some conventual buildings for Franciscan friars were started next to it, but these were still incomplete when a Williamite mob demolished them and the chapel, very soon after the 'Glorious Revolution' had put William and Mary in power. Full details of the brick and stone church, along with plans for rebuilding both the church and the convent, have luckily survived. The church was cross-shaped, 95ft long inside and with shallow transepts containing a Lady chapel and a chapel of St Francis. In each chapel the altarpiece had two Corinthian pillars to flank its picture, while four such pillars adorned the high altar with its picture of the risen Christ appearing to St Mary Magdalene. All three altars had 'other carved works answerable'; one thinks not of the opulent Flemish baroque of James II's Catholic chapels at Whitehall and Windsor, but of something more soberly conceived, in the vein of Wren's altarpieces in his London churches.

QUEEN ANNE AND EARLY GEORGIAN

The opening years of the eighteenth century saw Birmingham builders at work on some pleasing public buildings in the ancient street which formed the market place of the original town in the parish of St Martin's. More significant, and soon leading to an important architectural result, was the steady outward growth of the elegant, long residential district which came to be styled the 'High Town Quarter'.

The two best buildings in the old town were sited in the middle of the street. The Old Cross, already giving arched cover for a butter market, reached its final form in 1703. Its upper room was capped by boldly modillioned eaves, while the high-pitched roof, with its cupola girt by a square of railings, was much in the manner of many Dutch Renaissance town halls and weigh-houses, or of the strongly Netherlandish Custom House at King's Lynn. Higher up the street the somewhat smaller Welch Cross, likewise with a cupola and a bold weather-vane, was built in 1706.

By the middle of Queen Anne's reign Birmingham had just under 1,000 houses in its 'lower parish'. In the 'upper parish', on the beginning of the plateau and out towards Steelhouse Lane, there were between 700 and 800. Building and population growth were sure to occur in this direction. The entire parish, Dissenters apart, was outgrowing St Martin's. A new church was needed and was soon provided.

The Act of Parliament which allowed the creation of the new Birmingham parish and the building of its church, was passed in 1708; its prologue mentioned the 'great trade and commerce' of Birmingham which had become so populous that neither worship nor decent burial was possible, for most of the populace, in the church of St Martin. The inhabitants therefore desired to have a new church. The Act enabled them to go ahead and appointed not more than twenty commissioners and supervisors to carry out the work. The chosen plot was sold to the commissioners by Mrs Elizabeth Philips, and it was from this family, and not because of any special local devotion to St Philip, that the new church got its dedication. Predictably enough in Queen Anne's time, most of the commissioners were drawn from the Warwickshire gentry. Among them, with his roots deep in the Midland squirearchy, was the talented 'gentleman architect' Thomas Archer, who got out the designs for the church which was started in 1709 and which was complete, bar the top of its tower, in 1715.

St Philip's was the first of Archer's three churches, started before his association with Hawksmoor as one of the New Churches Commissioners of 1711. Its plan, a straight-forwardly basilican nave with aisles, and originally with no more than a shallow sanctuary, comes closer to Wren's more conventional parish church plans than to the daring spatial interiors, with their kinship to Hawksmoor's London churches, which Archer later achieved in Westminster and Deptford. The aisled and galleried nave has arcades with simple squared and fluted Tuscan piers; the undersides of the arches are embellished with coffering and rosettes. Fine panelling and an altarpiece, in the baroque taste, once graced the sanctuary. St Philip's, with no medieval building to replace and no concession needed to any Gothic predecessor, was a pre-Palladian building, quite like St Paul's which was started, a few years later, in Sheffield. Baroque detail, if not spatial planning, could reasonably be expected, and it was on the exterior that Archer notably applied it. Unlike the other architects then at work in England, Thomas Archer had first-hand knowledge of Rome in which, not long before his visit, Borromini had been a recognised master. Archer was not afraid to use Roman baroque detail. In St Philip's it appears in the concave-sided, boldly bracketed steeple which rises above a pedimented western feature, and still more in the Borrominian doorways and richly edged oval windows which give distinction to the ends of the aisles.

The tower and the ribbed dome of St Philip's were finished, with financial aid from George I, in 1725. By then the physical expansion of Birmingham had continued and many houses, along with a few buildings for public purposes, had been finished in the pre-Palladian, vernacular style still prevalent in many English provincial towns.

One attractive development had, indeed, been started before Queen Anne's death in 1714. East of Bull Street, in an area later slashed through by Joseph Chamberlain's Corporation Street, the Old Square was started in 1713; with its sixteen houses it was a miniature version of the much larger Queen Square in Bristol. It was a charming little piece of formal urbanism, with roads leading out at the middle of each side and a palisaded, geometrically designed central plot with clipped trees standing sentinel around it. Its houses, like nearly all those built at this time in central Birmingham, were of deep red brick with stone dressings. Their most striking feature lay in the high-plinthed, giant Doric pilasters, which marked the eight corners where the roads broke the square's terraced sequences. Giant pilasters of this type also existed, along with a fine baroque doorway adorned by a broken pediment and a flaming urn, in the Old Court House off High Street.

Other Birmingham houses built about this time displayed sturdy variations of verna-cular, craftsmen's baroque. In Jennens Row, near Mass House Lane, an early Georgian house had a shell-headed doorway, a fanciful, urn-capped feature in the middle of its parapet, and over its windows one of the numerous, characterful arrangements of plain or simply incised voussoir blocks found in Birmingham and other west Midland towns. Fancifully patterned stones, round three sides of its segmentally headed windows, lent character to Galton House in Steelhouse Lane. Closer to St Philip's, and overlooking its churchyard, Temple Row was started, in about 1719, in what was later called 'the highest and genteelest part of the town'; unlike many other Birmingham streets and squares it long kept its residential character, with its rooms and backyards free of the forges and workshops which marred the residential tone of areas once laid out solely as living quarters. Temple Row's houses were pleasant, restrained, pre-Palladian works; a fine doorway with a swan's neck pediment survived till late in the 1950s.

Likewise overlooking St Philip's churchyard, at first in brick with figures over its doorway but later heightened and refaced, the Blue Coat School was started in 1724. More important, down near New Street's eastern end, was the replacement of the timber-framed late medieval Guild Hall which had long housed King Edward VI's School. By a re-application of medieval guild and chantry funds this school had existed since 1552. Rebuilding started in 1708, but the main replacement of the ancient building was in 1731 and 1732. A three-sided court, on a plan then favoured alike for schools and almshouses, looked out onto New Street. Above the central doorway and the first-floor niches, a tall clock tower with a cupola surmounting it, conspicuously adorned Birmingham's skyline. In one stage a niche with rich baroque side-brackets held a statue of Edward VI. The whole brick and stone composition was attractive in its provincial, non-Palladian manner; the urns above the parapet were added in 1756. The designer-builder was a local mason named John Willinger. The carpenter, who also received considerable sums, was Jonathan Johnson who re-used much timber from the older building—an expedient which caused great trouble before a hundred years were out. The 1730s did not see the end of the Georgian work done on King Edward's for in 1747 the Flemish-born sculptor Peter Scheemakers sent two designs for marble chimney-pieces from London. One was to cost £80, the other £110; each was to include a bust of Edward VI. The less expensive design was rendered, of white marble with side brackets, a small pediment, and on top the young king's bust; it was Birmingham's main architectural detail by a master of such national standing. Then in 1752 the time came to fit up the school's library. William and David Hiorn, of the well-known Warwick family of designer-builders, made estimates for work which was carried out in a sober classical manner; William received payments till 1756.

Religious buildings were not overlooked at this time of Birmingham's steady expansion. More Nonconformist chapels, including the New Meeting of 1732, were built and an upper, or clerestory set of windows was placed, next year, over the nave of St Martin's. In Deritend, still in Aston parish though now much integrated with the old town of Birmingham, the medieval chapel of St John, standing close by the ancient four-arched bridge over the Rea, was replaced in about 1735 by the balustraded tower and box-like nave of a new chapel; its interior details, unlike those of a chapel of ease soon built in Birmingham itself, were staidly Roman Doric. When in 1749 the time came for a chapel to be built in the eastern portion of St Martin's parish, the new St Bartholomew's was a simple rectangular building, with two tiers of side windows, a trio of western doors, and a charming cupola. Outside, and within its aisled nave where Ionic eastern pilasters kept company with high-plinthed, Roman Doric nave pillars, the chapel clearly owed much to Gibbs' Oxford Chapel (now St Peter's, Vere Street) in Marylebone, and through that chapel to the same architect's more famous St Martin's in the Fields. William and David Hiorn probably designed St Bartholomew's; they were certainly responsible for the fine cedarwood altarpiece set up in 1753.

LATER EIGHTEENTH CENTURY

In 1758 a landowner named John Perrott built a belvedere, or look-out tower, on a lofty, unimpeded site in Edgbaston, west of Birmingham. It came to be known as Perrott's Folly and still stands as one of the city's more pleasing Georgian buildings. It is now closely hemmed in by roads and by some little groups of humble Victorian housing. When new, a slender brick-built octagon with a rounded stairway, 'church-warden' Gothic windows and rococo plasterwork in the ceiling of its main viewing room, it stood alone in open country with fine views over the still rural expanses of southern Staffordshire. Among the countryside stretches which Perrott and his friends could see was a desolate track of Handsworth parish which was soon transformed by the most memorable pioneer among Birmingham's factories.

The story of the Soho Manufactory brings us to one of the greatest among many notable men in Georgian Birmingham. A key point about Matthew Boulton is that he took an early, massive step towards the production of varied goods not in houses or in the small backyard workshops of local custom, but in a factory, not at first using steam power or machines yet gathering many workers, and many processes, on a single site. In 1761 he started his search for a suitable place. He found it, 2 miles north-west of Birmingham, in the desolate countryside of Handsworth Heath. Its only house, on a hill above the valley of the Hockley Brook, had once been a warrener's hut. The stream, already spanned by a watermill and with potentiality for damming and hence for water power, recommended this Soho site. Boulton soon started work; by 1765 his factory, with a housing colony for some of his workers, stood ready for use. Soho, as Boulton refashioned it, had ornamental charms as well as industrial importance, for Boulton, to quote Stebbing Shaw the Staffordshire historian, 'joined taste and philosophy with manufactures and commerce'. Like William Champion at his Warmley copper works near Bristol, Boulton turned a water-powered factory into an ornamental estate. Below the actual works a large artificial pool became, with skilful planting, a lake like those in many gentlemen's parks. Irrigation helped his workers in their specially built houses to make more of their garden plots. The factory, replacing the old watermill and with a long, narrow mill pond above it, had its buildings grouped round five spacious squares. Some of them appear to have been simple enough, but an engraving shows that one had a pedimented central block and at least one flanking pediment, while the main building was of more architectural pretension. A lunette stood over a spacious doorway in the centre of the façade, while the peaked central roof with its cupola, apparently rose over a polygonal central space. The block was of three main storeys with flanking pediments.

On the hill overlooking the newly industrialised Hockley valley, where the Victorian steeple of St Michael's church is now the most conspicuous building, Boulton built Soho House as his home, improving it with such novel devices as heating ducts and water closets. He finished it in 1799, ten years before his death. His architect for new reception rooms and probably for the mansion's ornamental front with its Ionic giant pilasters and its semi-circular Ionic porch, was Samuel Wyatt, an elder brother of the better known James Wyatt and a member of a large and prominent Staffordshire dynasty of architects and builders. Matthew Boulton, himself with a Staffordshire background, was employing a local man on this Soho commission. Samuel Wyatt became

Boulton & Watt's regular architect; in 1790 James Watt commissioned him to design his simply detailed house of Heathfield elsewhere on Handsworth Heath.

In the 1770s Boulton employed nearly 1,000 workpeople at Soho. Though Birmingham was, and remained, a stronghold of the small business and the backyard workshop, a few concerns had, by the time of the Napoleonic war, attained a fair size and needed large buildings. Among them was the factory of Edward Thomason, an apprentice of Boulton who struck out on his own as a button maker, and who followed Boulton as Birmingham's leading medal maker. The range of his distinguished clients was vast, and he was the first Birmingham industrialist to become a knight. His memoirs and his mural tablet in the cathedral show that this tireless tuft-hunter obtained many foreign decorations, and that he was vice-consul in Birmingham for no less than nine states. His factory had a façade of varied, consciously architectural design.

Thomason's factory stood at the corner of Church Street and Colmore Row. Church Street, and others near it, were among those lined by Birmingham's best late eighteenth-century domestic architecture. The systematic 'improvement' of the town was now projected. Acts of Parliament passed in 1769 and 1773 provided for better lighting and cleanliness in the central streets, and for the widening of some highways, particularly near New Street, Moor Street, and Colmore Row. The lack of space for the market sadly led, in 1784, to the pulling down of the older and finer of the town's two pillared crosses; in 1789 a new bridge was started over the Rea at Deritend.

Much had now been done to give Birmingham a better stock of late Georgian houses. Their style, as one would expect, was the chaste Greco-Romanism of the Adam taste diffused by pattern books and easy for provincial builders to render. Delicate neo-classical reliefs, with typical roundels, sphinxes, and winged lions, thus adorned a fireplace in Temple Street, while a room in Union Street once had a fine fireplace in the same taste. Typically delicate Adamesque fanlights and doorways lent distinction to a row of houses in Great Charles Street. In the enclosure of St Paul's Square, built about 1770 to 1780 to surround its church, a few late Georgian houses still survive on three sides; a doorway which has disappeared had the garlands of husks, draped to link three Grecian urns, which their builders could have copied from pattern books. Other Birmingham houses of these decades had more local and distinctive touches of design.

These features can, or could, be seen in several of Birmingham's late Georgian houses of brick and stone. Along with doorways having open pediments or Adamesque garlands, the more important windows were vertically divided into three main sections. The middle one might be capped by a miniature pediment, or else could be round-headed as in a 'Venetian' window. The window sections were parted from each other by the slenderest of pillarets, Roman Doric as were the tall, slim pilasters which marked the outer edges of the windows. Such windows were put up in Great Brook Street, in a house not far away in Woodcock Street, in Dale End, and in the house in Broad Street (whose main doorway is now Victorian Romanesque) which contains the Weights and Measures Office. Windows of this type adorn the front of the graceful late Georgian house at Five Ways, which marks the fork between Harborne and Calthorpe Roads and the beginning of the Edgbaston estate. They were used again in another elegant quarter on the other side of Birmingham. This was at Ashted, where the well known local physician Dr Ash had built a mansion; he was also the chief founder of the General Hospital whose severely simple first block was started soon after 1765 and finished after several delays. When Dr Ash retired to Bath in about 1788, his

14

estate was soon developed as a select suburb, being planned 'with more uniformity and regularity' than was usual in Birmingham. Dr Ash's house, with the curious addition of a cupola in the Wren manner, over a curved projection at the back, became a chapel for the inhabitants. The estate surveyor was named Kempson, and he so laid it out that the streets were from 48ft to over 60ft wide. A large crescent of two dozen houses, to stand on each side of the mansion turned chapel, was planned for the estate. In Ashted Row more windows of the individual Birmingham type were duly inserted. So too, as in hundreds of local houses both then and in the coming century, were window heads of a type which seems peculiar to Birmingham's late Georgian building tradition. The window heads curve up in a gentle ellipse, while over that curved shape a thin moulded hood has a small keyblock in the middle and then turns down at each side, to a small rectagular terminal block.

The proposed crescent at Ashted was not Birmingham's only formal late Georgian scheme. In 1790 a plot in Summer Hill was staked out for an 'elegant and uniform' terrace of fifteen houses. Two years earlier, and before the French revolutionary war 'laid the spirit of building', a project had been started, between the town and the suburban beginnings of Edgbaston, for a really monumental urban feature.

Birmingham had grown, by now, to a large town by current English standards. As its local historian Hutton pointed out, a 'pitiful market town . . . by pure industry, surpasses most of our cities.' This was about 1783; a survey of 1785–6 showed that the main town, excluding its outlying parts and Deritend, had nearly 10,000 houses and a population reckoned at over 53,000. The entire urban area may well have had over 60,000 people, more than twice the number in Bath and well on the way to surpassing Bristol. The central districts had little room for many more inhabitants, so growth now started on the outskirts. The more eminent and prosperous people sought semi-rural sites, as in Moseley or Edgbaston, for fair-sized mansions. Closer in, a little beyond the site of the japanner and printer John Baskerville's house space was found for a crescent of the dignity and elegance more normally associated with London or Bath.

Birmingham's crescent, with a simple terrace running back at each end, was started on an artificially raised platform of which one end survives to recall a frustrated venture. The occupants could look down a gentle slope to the canal wharves, and so over open country. The great terrace was to be nearly 1,200ft long and was to have twenty-three houses. Its architect was John Rawsthorne, once a pupil of James Wyatt. In some aspects of his design he seems to have remembered Bath, particularly in his giant Ionic pilasters like those in Lansdown Crescent, and in the ornamental treatment of his backward-sloping end pavilions which recalled the returned ends of Bath's Royal Crescent. Paired Ionic pilasters were to appear, at intervals, along the simpler sections of his crescent's front, while the projecting, very grand, middle house was to have a rusticated base, five windows in each floor, and an ornamental attic block with garlanded panels and on top a sculptured sphinx. The crescent was still being built in 1804, and in another eight years only a little more than half of it was complete.

Larger educational and cultural buildings were now put up. The small early Georgian Blue Coat School was replaced between 1792 and 1794, when Rawsthorne designed the severe, stone-faced, pedimented block which looked west over St Philip's churchyard until the 1930s. The town's first subscription library went up in 1780 and was replaced in 1793 by a larger building designed by William Hollins. He was self-trained, had studied Vitruvius with great care, and although he refused an invitation to work for the Tsarist court, he did send designs for a new mint in St Petersburg.

A riverside Vauxhall, or pleasure garden, had existed at Duddeston in 1758. The theatre had now started its career in Birmingham, though not yet in a purpose-built or permanent building. One had opened about 1730, and there were three, in make-shift quarters, in the 1740s; of these only that in Moor Street still played in 1751. Next year, a permanent theatre was built on part of the site of New Street Station. In 1774 it was enlarged, and in the same year a more important, architecturally more beautiful playhouse was built in New Street itself. Matthew Boulton and John Fothergill his business partner were among the proprietors who started meeting in 1773. Another was Thomas Saul, a local builder who erected, and may also have designed, the new theatre. The proprietors' minutes do not suggest that other theatres, in London or Bristol, were visited for hints on design, and no picture survives to show the auditorium of what may well have been a theatre of some importance. For its eventual exterior we are, however, better placed. Though an attempt of 1777 to get a Royal Licence was rebuffed, the owners must have felt it safe to build a monumental façade onto New Street. Boulton, who may already have employed Samuel Wyatt at Soho, recommended him as a suitable designer for a street elevation. Wyatt's design, along with some changes in the theatre's ground plan, was finished by 1780. Pictures show that it was a refined composition of an open arcade, an upper loggia of Ionic columns, and windows not unlike those noted in houses of about the same time. Paterae and medallion busts of Shakespeare and Garrick completed the composition. When in 1792 the auditorium was burnt out, Samuel Wyatt's frontage survived as one of New Street's best adornments. The new theatre, by George Saunders the county surveyor of Middlesex who had written a treatise on theatres, had iron columns and two tiers, each of sixteen boxes. This theatre got the Royal Licence in 1807.

More churches and chapels, of various denominations, were needed as Birmingham's population increased, and as streets and houses spread over what had been open country. In 1772 an Act of Parliament allowed the building of two new chapels of ease. One was St Mary's, started in 1774 on a site given by Mrs Mary Weaman whose Christian name became the church's dedication. Its round tower, with a needle spire rising over a Gibbsian composition, was finished in the initial building operation. More remarkable, in this building by Joseph Pickford of Derby, designer of Wedgwood's Etruria pottery works, was the octagonal body of the church, with two tiers of windows and in its eastern wall a pair of Venetian windows below a pediment.

More conventionally shaped, and still the central feature of the down at heel, once residential square which bears its name, was St Paul's which was started in 1777, to designs by Roger Eykyn of Wolverhampton. Samuel Wyatt suggested some changes and the steeple, probably to be as Gibbsian as that of St John's in Eykyn's home town, was not built. But the rectangular body of the church is strongly influenced by Gibbs' various designs for St Martin's in the Fields. The south-western and north-western doorways, and the two tiers of side windows, came very close to Gibbs' designs of over fifty years before; they also compare closely with features in the somewhat earlier Georgian church in Wolverhampton. The interior, with its plain rib and barrel vaults and Ionic pillars, is much simpler than in the London St Martin's, with plaster decoration more in the Adam taste of the time when the church was built. A fitting touch, in a church meant to serve many workers in the toy trade, is in the little enamel

16

number plates, white with a border of blue feathering, which adorn the pews. More spectacular, baroque in spirit and one of the finest things in Birmingham, is the richly toned east window by the local craftsman and glass painter Francis Eginton and copied from a large painting by Sir Benjamin West. Eginton had first worked at Soho as the head of Boulton's japanning department; he later worked on his own. Here in St Paul's the subject of his window is St Paul's persecution of the Christians and his conversion near Damascus. The window is somewhat later than the church. Francis Goodwin's completion of the steeple, with its graceful spire resting on an octagonal main stage which has alternating windows and Ionic pillarets, came in 1823.

Birmingham was now well provided with Nonconformist chapels and that of the Swedenborgians, opened in 1791, was the first ever erected by that particular body. A renewed, successful effort was also made to provide the town's Catholics with a reasonably central and permanent church. St Peter's, a little way off Broad Street amid some good late Georgian houses, was built in 1786, five years before the Act which legalised Catholic places of public worship. The plain, rectangular brick chapel had therefore to be unassertive, built to look like one of the town's many workshops, and with the windows and doorways on its street side less 'churchy' than those seen in 1969 when the church was pulled down. Inside, however, the three-sided gallery (its classical pillars were a Victorian renovation), the fine centrepiece for its chandelier, and the sanctuary fittings, more closely revealed the purpose of the building.

In 1791 Birmingham had its fierce and fiery experience of popular riots, anti-Jacobin in their first impetus and beyond the local constables' control. Nonconformist chapels, and the houses of Joseph Priestley and other Nonconformists and sympathisers with the French Revolution, were gutted. Their replacements apart, the riots had another architectural result. The disaster had proved, as did other disturbances in the Luddite and Reform Bill periods, that with the lack of a proper police force serious riots could only be put down by troops, often summoned from some distance. So barracks were built on the outskirts of some industrial towns. Those at Birmingham, quickly started in 1792 in the Ashted area and designed by Rawsthorne, cost £13,000 and had room for 162 cavalrymen and their horses. They had three-storey, pedimented blocks very typical of those in barracks elsewhere in the country; the Royal Arms, predictably enough, featured in the principal pediment.

The year 1792 saw the peak of the great canal mania. Canals, with their locks and little bridges, had already reached Birmingham making their own contribution to the town's architecture and opening up sites along their banks for new warehouses and factories. The Birmingham Canal, running in from Wolverhampton and its own junction with the Staffordshire & Worcestershire Canal, had been the first, being authorised in 1768 and completed four years later. The Birmingham & Fazeley, whose picturesque sequence of locks not far north of the middle of the modern city has lately been renovated, came next and linked the older canal with the Coventry Canal and other waterways east of Birmingham. The Worcester & Birmingham, whose enabling Act was passed in 1791, was in one way exceptional, for where it passed through the Edgbaston estate no commercial or industrial building was allowed on its course; the landlords thus assured the elegant, low-density residential growth of what soon became a truly beautiful suburb. The last canal to come into the Georgian town was the Warwick & Birmingham, allowed by Parliament in 1793 and finished a few years later. Not far before its end, amid a complex of basins and wharves behind Digbeth, it crossed the Rea by a seemly little three-arched aqueduct still visible from Fazeley Street if one looks over the high parapet of the river bridge. A more public canal building, originally put up to serve the waterways of the Birmingham Canal Company but also near the Gas Street terminal basin of the Worcester & Birmingham, was the Navigation Office which stood till 1913. Its main building was octagonal, with a central chimney stack and a dignified double stairway leading to its main entrance. It had, in its engagingly vernacular exterior, some idioms recalling a time earlier than its building date. Its rusticated window heads had a Gibbsian feeling, and the window above the main doorway had a baroque touch in its swan's neck pediment. Shallow archways below lunettes marked the entrances by which waggons could approach the wharves, while the wings, curving outwards and with Venetian and other windows seem, from an early print, to have been added later than the original building date.

By the time of the first census in 1801 Birmingham was growing fast, was wholly committed to the Industrial Revolution, yet was without any local government system fuller than that of any rural parish; effective power lay largely with the commissioners under the Improvement Act of 1769. The population of the old parish was 60,822, with nearly 12,000 in Aston. The same year saw the passing of another Improvement Act whose Street Commissioners ran Birmingham till it became a Municipal Borough.

REGENCY AND REVIVALISM

The Public Offices in Moor Street were Birmingham's first version of a proper town hall. The magistrates and the Street Commissioners shared the building which was put up between 1805 and 1807. It was designed by Hollins and had to be altered and extended about 1829, but in its main essence it remained, with a fine glazed dome over the principal staircase, and with Hollins' street elevation, till the time of its demolition. Its classical façade was very well composed, somewhat in the manner of James Wyatt's library at Oriel College, Oxford. It was, however, more lavish than that building, with paired and fluted Ionic half columns (those at Oriel are single and unfluted) and with balustrading below its main windows and above its cornice on each side of an attic block.

Hollins had other Birmingham commissions at about the same time. In Union Street he designed a new subscription library, also a dispensary whose plain Grecian Doric façade, with its plaster or Coade stone relief of Hygeia and a pot of herbs, survived till recent years. Mr Tudor Edwards has also attributed to Hollins the design of an 'Egyptian' conduit head (see his *Birmingham Treasure Chest*, 1953). The pseudo-Egyptian vogue was running during Hollins' career; the idiom appeared elsewhere, in Soho Road, in some doorway columns and fluted pilasters. Mr Edwards also suggests that Hollins may have designed the charming, now sadly demolished, almshouse enclosure in Deritend which was known as The Retreat.

House building, for dwellers with various incomes, went on apace in these early nineteenth-century decades. In the working class areas many of Birmingham's confined courts had been built by the 1830s. Approached from streets by narrow alleys, they were badly drained, and laid out on the back-to-back system but as a rule without cellar dwellings. A few old houses had become tenements and some bad housing, much liable to flooding, existed down by the Rea. Birmingham's housing may not, however, have been as grim as that of some quickly expanded northern towns. At the other end

18

of the social scale, terrace and villa development went on in Edgbaston, particularly along Calthorpe and Hagley Roads, and a little later along Bristol Road where one house of this time has verandah ironwork with Doric columns pierced in an imitation of classical fluting. Nor were elegant villas confined to Edgbaston. On one edge of the jewellery quarter, the upper end of Frederick Street has a pair of houses whose ground floor is well adorned with a row of five pairs of Greek Doric columns. Moseley Road was another major highway lined with villa-type houses, some stuccoed and others of plain brick. The best section of this road is at its Bordesley and Highgate Park end, where the road curves gently in front of a charming Regency sequence of houses, some with rounded stuccoed fronts and others of brick. Slim columns, open pediments and leaf or palmette capitals appear among the external adornments · of these neat little villas. Back in the middle of the town some streets, domestic in character and scale, had some houses also used as offices. In an area where sophistication and elegance were the rule, Waterloo Street, running west from St Philip's churchyard and hooking back to Colmore Row, contained some excellent houses. Their columns and other decoration combined Grecian detail, pseudo-Egyptian touches, and some more lavish and ornate plasterwork which foreshadowed Victorianism. Intersecting Waterloo Street, Bennett's Hill had houses in a simpler, less assertive but most pleasing style. Some were used as offices, and in some of the more important among them there was work by Charles Edge, from 1827 one of Birmingham's busiest architects.

When William Smith wrote about Birmingham in his history of Warwickshire of 1830, he had some good things to say of the town; his material must largely have been gathered a few years before his publication date. Smith says that Birmingham 'boldly solicits the ingress of the winds from each point of the compass', adding the opinion that 'the greater part of the houses are, in appearances, of a highly creditable description'. He also admits, in a good summing up both of the town's residential and more ceremonial aspects, that 'public structures' were restricted in size and shape by Birmingham's 'lack of corporate status'. Industrial, business, and religious architecture was, however, little affected.

Canals, still the basis of coal-fired industrialism, had a further architectural contribution to make before the railways overshadowed them. Birmingham's main new canal work was Telford's deep, direct cut which, between western Smethwick and Birmingham itself, straightened the boatmen's course and reduced the number of locks they needed to pass. It was a major piece of excavation, and where main roads crossed it important bridges were built. Galton Bridge, the masterpiece among them, is in Smethwick and so lies outside my scope. But Lee Bridge, taking the Dudley road over Telford's waterway, may also have been built to his design. Dated MDCCCXXVI (1826) and running slantwise over what was once a busy commercial waterway, it is an imposing piece of brickwork with pierced iron railings. The renewal of earlier bridges also came into Telford's programme. Delicately traceried iron bridges, dated 1827 and inscribed by the Horseley Iron Works, thus spanned the waterway.

Factory architecture tended to lag between the stylishness of Soho and the more pretentious efforts of the Victorians. But here and there simple industrial buildings display the refined taste of much Regency domestic building. In Granville Street an electrical concern now occupies a late Georgian factory range which has a good, simple entrance archway, while another late Georgian factory, with slightly recessed windows and iron glazing bars, contrasts with the more ornate, if more amusing industrial architecture elsewhere in the same street. In the jewellery quarter the Victoria works, at the corner of Frederick and Graham Streets, have another simple entrance, with a main portal and flanking doorways in the severe late Georgian manner, while not far away in Regent Street a workshop stands gracefully, with simple rounded walls, on a corner with Vittoria Street whose name came from Wellington's Spanish victory in 1813.

By the time of the Napoleonic War Birmingham had become a major centre of the gun trade. At the height of the war, and of Wellington's Peninsular campaign, the local gunmakers planned to set up a gun barrel proof house in their own town. The necessary Act was passed in 1813; later that year work started on one of early industrial England's best purpose-built establishments. The site, on the edge of a canal basin and thus easy for waterborne transport to London and elsewhere, was then open and picturesque. A courtyard, with its front railings curving out in a gentle sweep, looked out over canal basins and more or less open country. The long, terrace-like main building was of brick; the actual proving occurred in various sheds at its back. The designer-builder was John Horton of Deritend. The main glory of his work, between two rainwater heads boldly dated 1813, is the slightly projecting central element. The Roman Doric doorway and its architrave are a little earlier in feeling than their Regency date. Earlier still in its idiom is the lavish, richly coloured trophy of arms, baroque in spirit and akin to that placed nearly a century earlier in the great pediment of the noble Guildhall at Worcester. Inside, various features accord more closely with the building's date. Some iron banisters have a curious, flamelike pattern in their design. Upstairs, the boardroom has a plain marble fireplace, typically Regency doorways and, a later touch, a grisaille ceiling plaque whose arms repeat those over the outer doorway. A fine wall decoration displays the arms of William IV and Queen Adelaide. The paintings, dated 1835, were done by a herald painter named Thorp.

By the 1820s Birmingham was caught in a wider conflict of architectural revivalism. Some of its new buildings were classical in style. Others displayed the largely Perpendicular idioms of the early Gothic revival. The town was also, for several years, the home and working place of one of the most important late Georgian exponents of architectural bilingualism.

Thomas Rickman was not only a practising architect; he also wrote on architecture. As one of the first who seriously distinguished between the English styles from Norman to early Tudor times, he was, as far back as 1817 when his *Attempt to Discriminate the Styles of Architecture in England* came out in book form, a more learned and knowledgeable exponent of Gothic than most other designers of his time. He was also an important pioneer in the structural and decorative use of cast iron. His early career was varied, and he took seriously to architecture as a spare-time pursuit while he worked in Liverpool as an insurance clerk. His first architectural jobs were in Liverpool, but his Birmingham interest started in 1818, and in 1821 he went to Birmingham to live. From then onwards he and his partners—Henry Hutchinson who died in 1831 and R. C. Hussey who in 1838 took over from Rickman—designed several Birmingham buildings of note. Some were churches, some were secular buildings, the stylistic balance being slightly tilted to Grecianism. St George's Church, of 1820-3, was Rickman's first Birmingham building, Decorated rather than Perpendicular, with less structural iron than in the architect's two Gothic churches in Liverpool, but with tower and tracery details which markedly recalled them. Next, again Gothic but aisleless, was the church at Erdington which was opened in 1824; the Watt Memorial Chapel at Handsworth was Perpendicular and plaster-vaulted. All Saints', of 1832–3 and Early English with tall corner spirelets, was another of the firm's Gothic buildings. Another, and one of the last by Rickman himself, was the church built in Gem Street to the memory of the devoted, energetic Bishop Ryder of Lichfield. It was designed in 1836, its best feature being its slender brick and stone tower, with corner pinnacles grouped round its octagonal top stage. But in St Peter's, Dale End, of 1825–7 and with its Greek Doric portico, and a bell turret modelled on the Athenian Tower of the Winds, Rickman and Hutchinson switched to the Greek Revival. They did the same, in 1826–9, at St Thomas' whose fine Ionic western feature of two curved colonnades and a central arch beneath a well composed tower, still stands despite the bombing of the actual church. Two secular buildings by Rickman were also classical, this time Corinthian. At the corner of Waterloo Street and Bennett's Hill the Birmingham (now Midland) Bank building of 1830 had two admirable frontages, while down in New Street, a year earlier, the Birmingham Society of Artists' Exhibition Rooms had a circular exhibition gallery and, at the main entrance, a most dignified four-columned portico with a gap between the plinths of its two middle pillars. It added another fine feature to what Smith called 'decidedly the best' street in the town. New Street had not, of course, been planned as a whole, but its individual buildings gave it quality. At its lower end James Wyatt's simple front of the Hen and Chickens Inn was new in 1800. At the top end a fine new church was soon built; between these two buildings some houses and shops, the artists' headquarters and the Theatre Royal's façade added to the interest of a street which soon saw the rise of a Gothic building of much note in architectural history.

Rickman's contribution apart, Birmingham's religious architecture continued to increase with the growth of the town. Another Catholic church, the forerunner of the present St Chad's on its sloping, none too long site, was started in 1806, a roomy but somewhat gaunt and boxlike late Georgian building. Not far away, in Steelhouse Lane, the Ebenezer Chapel of 1816–18 had what Smith called a 'handsome front' and was, for greater dignity, set well back from the road. The Jews built a larger synagogue in 1827 and a few more Anglican churches dated from the same decade. There was also, as in Moseley and Edgbaston, some enlargement of ancient, outlying churches whose parishioners had increased; at Moseley the alterations were by Rickman.

Of the new Anglican churches the most strikingly placed was Christ Church, finely sited up its impressive stairway at the corner of New Street and Colmore Row. An Act of 1803 authorised it, and George III gave £1,000 towards the cost. Its architect, a colleague of Rawsthorne, was Charles Norton and the church was completed by 1814. Despite mahogany in its altarpiece, pews and gallery fronts, its unaisled interior was gaunt and boxlike and the church's main merit lay in its western feature. There, the original plans were for four Ionic pilasters and for a domed Ionic cupola above the tower. But the influence of the London St Martin's prevailed; the actual church had a portico, and above it an octagonal stage and finally a spire.

Another important church was the first put up in the southerly district of Bordesley. This was the Commissioners' church of Holy Trinity, of brick faced with Bath stone, designed by Francis Goodwin and built in 1820–3. The style is pseudo-Decorated and the tracery, including that of the eastern rose window, is rendered in cast iron. The broad interior, galleried but structurally unaisled, was of some importance. More striking is the townscape impact of Goodwin's western façade, with tall pinnacles and a cavernous giant arch revealing delicate vaulting, carved stonework convincingly in the fourteenth-century manner, and a richly traceried window.

Among Nonconformist chapels the New Meeting Unitarian Church, replacing Priestley's chapel which the rioters of 1791 had burnt, was built in 1802. Smith allows it 'considerable architectural beauty', and there is much dignity in the pedimented façade with its row of paired Ionic pilasters. Since the 1860s the building has been a Catholic church. At the sanctuary end there have inevitably been changes, but most of the charming galleried interior, with much early seating, survives to serve the church's changed purpose. Close at hand, a really notable façade was that of Carr's Lane Congregational Chapel, built in 1819-20 as a successor to two earlier buildings. Its architect, S. T. Whitwell, was a Warwickshire man who had worked in the office of the London Docks and who also designed Birmingham's New Library in Temple Row. The plain side walls of his chapel survived an unhappy Victorian rebuilding of its façade in Lombardic Romanesque. But Whitwell's original frontage was a dramatic composition, with its dated attic block rising high behind a portal element whose triumphal arch, beneath a simple pediment, makes me wonder if Whitwell, with his earlier contacts in London, drew ideas from the published work of the very individual French architect Ledoux. He could certainly have taken ideas from Soane, whose lectures he had attended.

More unusually planned, though not without precedent, was the Mount Zion Chapel in Graham Street, built in 1823 by a Presbyterian preacher but soon handed over to the Baptists. Behind its fine Greek Doric portico it was an 'auditory' church, octagonal but with a circular shape for its beautiful circular dome. It seems that its designer may have got ideas from the recently built, very similar interior of St Chad's church at Shrewsbury. All these chapels were in the classical tradition still normal for the Nonconformists. But Gothic soon crept in, and at Erdington in 1835 a new Congregational chapel was given a façade in Rickmanesque Early English. Nor were ordinary churches the only religious buildings now erected. Cemeteries, separate from the churchyards, were now being laid out in England's large towns. Birmingham's first, at Key Hill, had a chapel by Charles Edge, built in 1834 as a small Greek Doric temple with a four-columned portico at each end.

Back in central Birmingham the Theatre Royal was again burnt, bar Samuel Wyatt's New Street frontage, in 1820. It was soon imposingly rebuilt, the architect being Samuel Beazley, a specialist in such buildings who had worked in London at the Lyceum and Drury Lane. Central Birmingham also saw the completion of the last two major buildings put up under the town's old municipal regime.

About 1815 the Street Commissioners built a new meat market, called Smithfield in the London manner, on the site of Birmingham's old moated manor house. The period was prolific for the building of covered markets, and Birmingham's old street market in the Bull Ring was soon replaced by one of England's largest buildings of this kind. The commissioners first discussed the scheme in 1824; their original intention was for a building combining a market, public offices and a concert hall. But an Act of 1828 allowed both for a market and a town hall. The market site, just west of the Bull Ring, was bought by 1831 and work started that year. Charles Edge was the architect, and in 1834 the work was finished. The roof was nearly 500ft long and the building, with its spacious, somewhat undramatic interior, was said to be the finest market hall in England. Its exterior was of high quality, with a rusticated and arcaded southern frontage and two Doric entrance façades. That at the Bull Ring end was the more imposing of the two, with offices and little shops on each side of its principal approach.

The next public building put up by the commissioners was the Town Hall. The site, a none too spacious, sloping rectangular plot, was bought in 1830. For the first time in Birmingham an architectural competition was held. Rickman and Goodwin competed, so too did Beazley the theatre architect and Charles Barry who soon found other work lower down New Street. But the choice fell on the young Joseph Aloysius Hansom, not yet known as the inventor of the Hansom cab but already with some architectural experience in Wales and the North. He was asked to consult Soane, and John Foster a prominent architect in Liverpool. In essence his design, for a large, peripteral Corinthian building, raised on an arched and rusticated podium and based on the Temple of Jupiter Stator in Rome, was confirmed, and the Town Hall as designed by Hansom and Welsh, his partner, was started in 1834.

The Town Hall's building story was chequered and, for Hansom, disastrous. The financial arrangements between the commissioners, their architects and the contractors led, early in 1834, to Hansom's bankruptcy. Foster was then asked to supervise the work, and in 1835 Charles Edge, with whom Hansom had worked two years earlier on drawings for the refitting of the gutted St Peter's, Dale End, was appointed architect. Under him the Town Hall, in use since 1834, was finished, and work continued at least till 1849. In 1834 its northern end had remained unfinished, and Edge's drawings show that at first he meant to give the back elevation four plain square piers with moulded capitals. Fortunately his backward lengthening fulfilled Hansom's idea of a hall completely girt with a fluted Corinthian colonnade. The interior, with its gallery on thin iron columns and with bold Corinthian pilasters, has been altered within the last half century, and the present ceiling is more opulently baroque and less in keeping with the main design, than the original covering. The main concert and meeting hall is imposing, if cramped; a greater defect is the building's small foyer space.

When the Town Hall was opened work was in hand on new Gothic buildings for King Edward VI's School. The story of the replacement of the early Georgian buildings starts in 1821. A committee then started to consider the school's obviously bad structural state. They asked Rickman to survey the school; his 'accurate and clear' report showed up its 'lamentably delapidated and dangerous' condition. Much trouble flowed from the re-use by the builders of the 1730s, of moulded beams and other timbers which must have come from the medieval Guild Hall which had once housed the school. Rickman considered that new buildings were essential; he and his partner Hutchinson soon submitted plans for new classical schools. Meanwhile they carried out stopgap repairs, particularly in 1824 when the fall into the courtyard of an arm from the royal founder's statue caused the removal of Edward VI, along with the urns perched above the balustrade. The choice of a site, and complications both with finance and the law, caused some years' delay, but in 1832 a competition was held and the numerous entries were sifted the following year. Goodwin came third; second was a little known Bath architect named Hayward, and the winner was Charles Barry.

Barry's design, minus a central oriel and a clock tower which were cut out to save expense, was carried out between 1834 and 1838. The buildings were quadrangular in plan, and allowed for the site's southward slope; the arcaded back cloister stood lower than the New Street façade. A two-storeyed corridor, with the building's most striking late Gothic detail, bisected the inner courtyard. St Peter's church at Brighton, and a church in Manchester, had already shown Barry as a Gothic designer, but his school at Birmingham was far more medieval in feeling. Yet it was, like the Houses of Parliament on whose drawings Barry worked while his Birmingham school was in progress, a classically symmetrical building in a convincingly Gothic dress. The New Street façade was a balanced composition in the classical manner, with a tall oriel at each end and a 'Perpendicular' doorway exactly in the centre. The omitted central oriel would have made the composition more impressive. So too, directly above it, would the clock tower, ornately tabernacled and pinnacled and rising high to a delicate *flêche*. Barry was probably disappointed at the loss of a central feature which would have been splendid, though difficult and costly to maintain; he soon found compensation in the basically similar central pinnacle above the middle of his Houses of Parliament.

The tracery in the school's windows was Perpendicular, and the interior detail was in the same late Gothic style. In the upper and lower corridors the wall panelling, and the ribbed and bossed vaulting, were specially well rendered in the manner of about 1500. Over the Great Hall the hammerbeam roof, a little more ornate than in Barry's drawings, was in the class of Wolsey's Hampton Court and Christ Church, Oxford. The whole building must have been a valuable exercise for what Barry soon designed for the new Palace of Westminster. The question remains—how far was Augustus Pugin, Barry's collaborator in the Houses of Parliament and employed by Barry about the time of the furnishing of the Birmingham school, responsible for any detail in King Edward VI School? He was in the area at this time when he did not disdain the Perpendicular style, and could have assisted Barry on some of the decorative work. It is said that he designed the simply framed honours board in Big School. More probably his work is the Chief Master's ceremonial chair with its canopy, linenfold panelling and the late Gothic lettering of the word SAPIENTIA very much in Pugin's manner.

The year 1838, when the new King Edward's School was occupied, and when Birmingham at last became a municipal borough, was important for the town's history and symbolic for its architectural future. The railway from London had by then reached the town which was soon to see one of the finest buildings of the early railway age. Pugin was now influentially in office as Professor of Ecclesiastical Antiquities in the newly built Catholic college out at New Oscott. For this, and for another church building in suburban Birmingham, we have to look back a short way into Gothic's pre-ecclesiological phase. The college's main building, by Robert Potter of Lichfield and started in 1835, had been built in the staid, serviceable educational late Tudor style much favoured at that time for such buildings; Pugin's additions, a Perpendicular apse in the chapel and an oriel in the entrance tower, were structurally unimportant. Nor was there much to foreshadow the ecclesiological movement in the new church of St George in Edgbaston. It was built, to designs by the Catholic architect J. J. Scoles, in 1836–8, being aisled, in a simple, pre-Tractarian Early English with slender pillars like those placed by Scoles, a little before, in the church for his own denomination in the London suburb of St John's Wood. But within the Gothic field Pugin and his associates were soon to triumph, while Birmingham swiftly expanded, with much disappointing architecture, as a great Victorian town.

HIGH VICTORIAN

The first forty years of Birmingham's full municipal life saw vast increases in the town's buildings but no marked improvement in the aesthetic quality of its architecture. The more pleasing buildings tended to date from the first dozen years after 1838. In any event, the sheer quantity of Birmingham's architecture of this period is so great that any study must use selectivity and a stern discipline of choice.

We may reasonably start with Augustus Pugin. Thanks to Potter's sound existing work he could do little with the existing buildings at New Oscott. Where he did leave his strong medieval mark was in his two brick and stone outer gateways of 1838 in the early Perpendicular of the late fourteenth century, with initials and insignia referring to Bishop Walsh who was then the Catholic Vicar Apostolic of the Midland District. The main gateway's design is said to owe much to that of Stoneleigh Abbey elsewhere in Warwickshire. It is certainly more typical of its architect's essentially English Gothic than the best known of his Birmingham buildings.

Plans for replacing the original late Georgian St Chad's went back to 1834 when Rickman made designs for a Gothic building whose twin-towered façade would have recalled the west front of York Minster. Then in 1838 Pugin designed a church, with a single tower but on a large scale. His actual St Chad's of 1839–41 has two spired towers as the western feature of a church on a steeply rising, none too long site, whose exterior is bulky and graceless and gives a Germanic or Belgian effect. Many decorative details are better than the architecture of a somewhat overrated church, whose cathedral status came in 1850. The lofty arcades with their slender pillars, and with capitals in the English late Gothic manner, are of much dignity and help to give the impression of a German hall church. The wide crossing supports no tower, and the church's eastern end consists of a dignified but cramped apse. A main difficulty, the more so since Pugin's church became a cathedral, was the lack of length imposed by its sloping site. Beneath the chancel a crypt was structurally necessary, and Pugin's crypt is neo-Norman, a style fairly popular in England while St Chad's was being built, but not one in which its architect normally worked.

Pugin's Decorated and Tudor Gothic nunnery at Handsworth was built while St Chad's was being finished. It was a fairly small, unobtrusive building, but a novelty, at such a date in England, for its frankly medievalist inspiration. The blue brick crosses and other details in buildings whose main material is red brick, recalled the architect's new gateways at Oscott. A little later, a Gothic building for corporate and religious purposes was put up near the Town Hall, in the busiest part of the town. Queen's College, chartered in 1843, was first a small medical school, but soon taught medicine along with theology and a few other subjects. Its quad, with a small Perpendicular chapel across part of its southern side, was by the local architects Drury & Bateman. The enclosure, with its somewhat distant Oxbridge reminiscences, was tall and severe, in brick and stone and in an early Tudor style. The main effect was reserved for the stone façade which was replaced, about 1900, by one of Birmingham's richest Flemish Gothic extravagances in pale terracotta. In its early form, with a central oriel and one at each side, it came close to what Barry had planned for King Edward VI School.

Along with these Gothic ventures Birmingham saw continuing, and at times splendid, assertions of the classical tradition. The new hospital in Bath Row, by Bateman &

Drury and built early in the 1840s, showed Queen's College's designers in a late Georgian vein, with four square piers instead of columns, supporting their porch. In Newhall Street, Elkington's electroplate factory had a simply classical façade with a Greek Doric porch whose recent demolition is an unpardonable loss. In Edgbaston, Charles Edge built his share of the villas and rows of houses which added to the district's well-spaced suburban charm. His drawings show a progression from Grecianism, through a Greco-Italian blend to a more complete exponent of Italianism. In villas his main Grecian details appeared in porches, but Ionic columns also added dignity to an occasional entrance hall.

More impressive, of the first three years of Victoria's reign, was the noble northern terminal block of the London to Birmingham Railway. The tracks ended nearer the street than those at Euston, so that the terminal building combined the functions both of the great hall at Euston and of the elder Philip Hardwick's Doric propylaeum. Here at Curzon Street, Hardwick used Ionic for the four-pillared colonnade which proudly adorns the office block. Flanking archways were in his original design, but one was soon replaced by the simple building of the railway hotel.

Curzon Street station was, however, inconveniently far from the town centre. The trouble was soon remedied by the building of the great station to the south of New Street on a site near King Edward VI's School. The station's main feature was its great single-span roof, with gently curving arches over 200ft across. The other buildings were of less architectural note than the Curzon Street station which they replaced.

Birmingham's canal architecture was now past its best, but along the canals many warehouses and factories were still being built. One of them, of 1837 and designed by a London architect named William Herbert, belonged to the British White Lead Company. It made an impressive grouping, its chimney arising from a monumental base, and a round-arched Italianate style for its canal-side portal and outer walls.

Victorian churches were inevitably numerous as the city grew. As in other towns, the Nonconformists mixed neo-classical and Italian Romanesque design with a growing amount of Gothic. It was, however, significant that one of their 'smartest' chapels, the Unitarian church of the Messiah, was ornately neo-Decorated with a strongly medievalist tower and spire contrasting sharply with the classical late Georgian steeple of its new neighbour (now Christian Scientist), a distinctive, excellent building by J. R. Botham with its colour contrast of stone dressings and the blackish-blue brick much loved by the engineers of the London & North Western Railway. J. J. Bateman designed this worshipping place but neither he nor any of the designers who worked for the established church, impinged much on the dominance of J. A. Chatwin.

Ecclesiological church building in Birmingham had indeed started under Pugin, soon followed by two churches by R. C. Carpenter—a special favourite among the prophets and patrons of that school. His church of St Andrew, uphill in Bordesley and well placed at the top of the road, was strictly ecclesiological, with a north-western tower which once had a spire, curvilinear tracery and a northern arcade alternating between round and octagonal columns. The same architectural ideas appeared a little later in the Catholic church at Erdington, with Charles Hansom, Joseph's younger brother, as its architect. It is strictly Decorated in style, lavishly adorned with foliate and figured sculpture, and with a tower and broach spire as its best features. Another Puginesque Gothic church is St Michael at Handsworth, conspicuously placed not far from Matthew Boulton's Soho House. Here too a tower and spire form the culmination of a church in the Decorated style, the only one in Birmingham by its architect W. Bourne. Edward Holmes (at Selly Oak) and the Martin-Chamberlain partnership were other designers of Birmingham churches in a period when it was more normal for new churches and alterations to existing buildings to be carried out by J. A. Chatwin.

Chatwin's churchbuilding dominance well illustrates Victorian Birmingham's practice whereby almost all available commissions went to local men. The city thus has, among its churches, no work by such national figures as Sir George Scott, Street or Butterfield. Pearson, with his nobly vaulted and apsidal St Alban's in Bordesley, and with his more modest St Patrick's not far away, was the only nationally eminent later Victorian church architect to get his chance in the city; St Alban's, though never given its intended tower and spire, is easily the best of Birmingham's Victorian churches. Those by J. A. Chatwin, though competent and respectfully within the Gothic conventions, are run of the mill revivalist work. His new nave and apsidal chancel at Aston, and his almost total rebuilding of St Martin's, are dignified Decorated achievements, while the new nave which he cleverly grafted onto Scoles' earlier nave and north aisle at St George's in Edgbaston, is more successful. His church of St Augustine, Rotton Park was ornate and of no great merit in its nave and apsidal chancel but more distinguished for the dignity of its tall southern tower and spire.

Chatwin had trained under Barry, and like his master he was no exclusive Gothicist. His versatility may explain the success of the baroque chancel which he added to St Philip's. In commercial jobs he was apt to be an Italianist. For example, on the western side of St Philip's churchyard is his building of 1864 for the Birmingham Joint Stock Bank, a rich little palazzo with its Doric and Corinthian façade. The Banks were staunch advocates of the Italian palazzo. Down in New Street an impressive building was that of the Birmingham & Midland at a corner near the station. Started in 1867, with an Ionic porch, an array of Corinthian pilasters and half columns, and with an ornately pilastered banking hall nearly 100ft long, it was and is more successful than its architect Holmes' Gothic work.

Parish churches were not the only buildings in Birmingham now put up in the ecclesiastical Gothic style. The chapel in the Church of England cemetery off Warstone Lane was remarkably elaborate, with its clerestory and a tower and spire, for a building of this type. More in keeping with the nature and purpose of its buildings was the Anglican Training College built, between 1850 and 1852, in the then semi-rural setting of Saltley; it was one of several Church of England teacher training colleges which were founded about this time. Benjamin Ferrey, a well established Puginian Gothicist, won the competition for its design. His original college was a single quadrangle with no chapel (though one was intended), with an impressive gateway which has a two-tiered oriel, an oriel-windowed lodge for the principal in the north-eastern corner, and across the college's eastern side a single-storey block which gave it an open-sided effect. In the cusping of its oriels, in its hall windows and in the austere little single-light windows which light its cubicles, the college's idiom was almost wholly the Decorated in vogue five centuries before its building. Across the city in the equally rural area of Moseley, another range of educational Gothic buildings was put up, in 1854–6, for the training of Nonconformist ministers. This was Spring Hill College which in another thirty years moved to Oxford, there taking its present name of Mansfield College. Its buildings, by a London architect named Joseph James, who won a competition for which twenty-five architects entered, are of brick and stone, and the style for the tower, windows, and other exterior and interior details, is a mixture of Decorated and of somewhat lavish Perpendicular. At Handsworth the Wesleyan Training College, opened in 1881, and by Ball & Goddard who may have been influenced by the Spring Hill college's plan, is wholly Perpendicular, with a finely pinnacled tower, low flanking ranges, and a loftier projecting block.

In the frontages of factories and warehouses the Victorian Renaissance designers had no monopoly. In the jewellery quarter, in Granville Street, and in Digbeth where what was originally an iron warehouse has an imposing doorway with a fancifully capped French Gothic tower, the mid-Victorian decades saw a multicoloured, sometimes vulgar, but often characterful selection of Gothic and round-arched medieval idioms. In the jewellery quarter the most challenging building is a turreted, Lombardic Romanesque industrial fortress, with red, creamy white and dark blue among the colours of its brickwork, as individual a building as any of the so-called 'Byzantine' extravagances of contemporary Bristol. The *rundbogenstil* (round-arched style) was likewise used by C. A. Edge, Charles Edge's son, when he planned additions to a factory by his father in Holloway Head, also at Small Heath, in the ceremonial façade, the side blocks and sturdy corner towers of the great factory of the Birmingham Small Arms Company. This dated from 1862 to 1866, its architect being Thomas Warner Goodman. The jewellery quarter has some Gothic façades of a somewhat Italian stamp. In Warstone Lane a small three-tiered façade is, for its size, of astonishing variety, while the great Hampton Street Works, built in 1872 by a Cadbury who made pearl buttons, exploits the same Gothic manner on a larger scale. Some of this factory's foliate details resemble those found in the educational buildings of J. H. Chamberlain. Already, in 1857, this same architect had used a fanciful Gothic style in the shop and office block which he built in Union Street.

Chamberlain, with his Ruskinian ideas and his enthusiasm for Italian medieval art, was a pioneer among Birmingham's decorators and architects. This was specially true in his schools and public buildings, but he was also an originator as one of many designers who worked on private houses. Out in Moseley he designed the lavish late thirteenth-century essay of Highbury which was Joseph Chamberlain's home, while in Harborne his reconstruction of William Kenrick's house was of sufficient note, as a study in Ruskinism, for its octagonal boudoir to be thought worthy of recent re-erection in the Victoria and Albert Museum. Charles Edge had his hand in Birmingham's growing Victorian villadom, while his son Charles Allerton Edge, with some extremely nasty Gothic villa designs in red brick and stone, seems to have been still more deeply involved. Nor was the city's middle class housing confined to the individual villas of the prosperous. Similar motifs, with Gothic doorways and fanciful window arcading, appeared in continuous rows of houses such as those in Arden Road in Aston. At a humbler level, but still for middle class occupants or the better paid manual workers, many tunnel-back houses, their backs approached by little tunnels cutting through from the streets, continued to be built. The back-to-back, and the courts of a less regulated type, were long inhabited by thousands of the poor; some back-to-backs were still being put up till the 1870s and the early days of bylaw housing. But houses of better standards, with street upon street of minuscule front plots and the strongly local feature of ground-floor windows sticking out on a rectangular plan, were customary by about 1880; the dates of 1877 and 1878 on houses in streets off Dudley Road, mark the trend. Little courts of no small charm with their feeling of secluded, non-vehicular enclosure, and with little front gardens running out towards central pathways, were another marked feature of late Victorian Birmingham, still found in the inner suburbs, whether in the area off Dudley Road or at Sparkhill.

Public buildings now increased in numbers and range. Before 1870 the state and the municipality bore little responsibility for the people's education, but voluntary endeavours, for both adults and children, were more prominent than before. An important building, across the road from the Town Hall and with its unfluted Corinthian half-columns well answering Joseph Hansom's colonnade, was the Birmingham and Midland Institute. It was built in 1855-7 to designs by E. M. Barry, for adult further education; its classical idiom was soon continued next door in the Central Library, where William Martin rendered, with internal changes, a scheme by the younger Barry. The staircase has been admired, perhaps too much, by Victorian enthusiasts; the main interior, after a bad fire in 1879, was renewed in the present form.

More important for an understanding of Martin & Chamberlain were the schools and other buildings put up, after the Education Act of 1870, for the Birmingham School Board; they made up a group of much note in the whole corpus of Birmingham Victoriana. Work started in the 1870s and extended well past the end of that decade, but many essentials of what was seen as a set of vital, spiritually uplifting buildings were soon established. Their towers, sometimes rising to fair heights and capped by wooden spirelets, were to be beacons of a new, municipally provided, enlightenment. The Martin & Chamberlain schools, most of them in the first few years to Chamberlain's designs, must have been a revelation to those who dwelt in the close-packed districts round them, particularly where the buildings, like those of the Oozells Street school which was opened in 1878 and the Floodgate Street school down by the Rea, had to be built high because of the smallness of their sites. The redness of their brickwork was apt, as in other buildings by the same firm, to be relieved by the durable colours of tile friezes, while window heads and spandrels were often filled, in a pioneering way which anticipated the curvatures of Art Nouveau, by free-flowing foliate and floral patterns. Chamberlain used this foliage particularly well in the imposing, three-gabled façade of the School Board's own offices.

Schools were not the only item in Martin & Chamberlain's extensive, eventually envied volume of municipal work. Police stations were among their jobs. So too, after a time when Charles Edge did some designs for the Birmingham Waterworks Company (taken over by the corporation in 1876), were some of the pumping houses of the new civic undertaking, impressive Italianate or Gothic palaces for the gleaming machines in their spacious halls. Some of these buildings have disappeared, and others were put up after 1880. One, however, goes back to the last years of the private company. This is the Edgbaston Pumping Station whose chimney rises high above one side of the Rotton Park reservoir, a slender campanile of a structure, impressive if slightly incongruous in Italianate Gothic, with an exotic iron balcony.

Not far from the School Board offices another educational building was also started in 1875, being opened within five years. This was Mason College, founded by the industrialist Sir Josiah Mason and later the original main building of the university. Photographs suggest that it was somewhat grim and uninspiring inside, but its façade made an imposingly windowed, arcaded and pinnacled northern side for the taut enclosure of Chamberlain Square. Carefully balanced, and more conventionally Gothic than some Chamberlain buildings, the college had a flavour of Scott's forebuilding at

St Pancras' station. Jethro Cossins, the founder of an important Birmingham practice, was the architect of Sir Josiah's choice.

Close to Mason College and the Town Hall, the long, ponderously Renaissance, slightly domed block of the Council House was started in 1874. Its architect was Yeoville Thomason, of the family which had earlier claimed Sir Edward Thomason the medallist. His local connection and his early training under Edge placed him well for a prosperous Birmingham practice. He had already worked, in clubs and commercial buildings, in a rich Renaissance style; his Council House was in the same tradition. Some such building was clearly needed for the growing, more efficient administration of the Joseph Chamberlain age. Ceremonially, and in its administrative capacity, the new Council House clearly served a good purpose. Yet when one compares it to such a classical masterpiece as Brodrick's Town Hall at Leeds it somehow fails to strike the right note. It is too long, as one sees in the otherwise fine sequence of its two upstairs halls, for its other proportions. Its central element is awkwardly composed, the dome is too small, and much of the Renaissance detail is heavy and coarse. It appears at its best when suddenly glimpsed along some narrow street, while its curved council chamber and its grand staircase are successfully imposing. It is hard to reckon Thomason as a designer of more than average capacity.

Birmingham's business and shopping centre had changed much by the late 1870s, from its late Georgian aspect. About 1875 a secluded addition to its shopping facilities was the Great Western Arcade, less extensive than Cardiff's series of such covered, pedestrian shopping thoroughfares, but agreeable and still a more pleasing sauntering place than the recent covered shopping complex off the Bull Ring. The architect, for an arcade whose idea was better than the foliate pilasters and ponderous Renaissance exterior motifs of its deail, was W. H. Ward.

The arcade runs parallel to Bull Street; near its lower end a really important new urban highway was soon started to give the city of Joseph Chamberlain and his reforming colleagues a direct, spacious link between New Street and the northern suburbs. Corporation Street, with J. H. Chamberlain as its surveyor, was started in 1878, driving ruthlessly through an older townscape, engulfing the down at heel Old Square and causing, as New Street station had done, the healthful demolition of streets and houses of disreputable slumdom. Two-dimensionally it was a better street than in the mixed quality of the buildings which lined it. A hotel by Yeoville Thomason, in what *The Builder* called a 'free Italian' style, with terracotta panels, was fittingly called The Chamberlain Arms; another lavish frontage, by William Doubleday, was that of the likewise politically named hotel, the Cobden. But Birmingham's impressive new street was an architectural disappointment, though at its top end a good plot was left available for a building which notably improved the city's taste.

TERRACOTTA AND ARTS AND CRAFTS

For the first half of the 1880s Birmingham's architecture continued much as before. Yeoville Thomason extended the Council House, with the addition of a bell tower, in the style which he had employed for the earlier building. Out at Erdington he also designed the Jaffray Hospital, a dull, undistinguished red brick jumble which was opened in 1885. Jethro Cossins continued as a Gothicist, and his fine apsidal chancel for Joseph Hansom's Catholic church of St Catherine of Siena was added in the 1890s.

The most striking new Birmingham church was that of the Redeemer, built by the Baptists on the Hagley Road. In so fashionable a district Gothic was the preferred style, so handled (as in some suburban Nonconformist churches elsewhere) as to give an appearance more like a strongly ecclesiological Anglican church than most Gothic churches so far built by the Nonconformists. The architect was a Londoner, James Cubitt who may have belonged to the capital's great building dynasty; his building was finished in 1882. It is cruciform in plan, and its shallow transepts with their wheel windows, its octagonal, originally pinnacled central tower, and its fine round-apsed sanctuary give the feeling of the church which a small French monastic community might have built about 1200. The church must have come as a shock to the Edgbaston of its own time for it was, and is, unlike any other place of worship in the city.

The volume of Martin & Chamberlain work continued unabated; more slim-spired board schools were built, with terracotta an increasing, but still subsidiary decorative material, while in the heart of the city one of Chamberlain's last buildings was the School of Arts and Crafts, unimposing inside despite a small aisled hall, but exciting outside with its array of gables, panels and windows of the normal Gothic shape, with rows of tiles, and also with the striking round window whose trellis pattern is over-laid by free-flowing stalks and leaves. It is the most individual of its designer's works, disregarding all normal ideas of tracery in a pattern akin to Art Nouveau.

More normal Victorian Gothic, presumably acceptable to many citizens, was seen in the gabled and spired memorial fountain which Chamberlain designed to honour Joseph Chamberlain who had, before its erection in 1881, completed his spells of mayoral office and made his mark in national politics. The memorial blended the concepts of an Albert Memorial and of an Eleanor Cross. Set up within the statesman's lifetime, in this respect it resembled one of the iron clock-towers, painted green and upholding their timepieces on slender pedestals of medieval or Renaissance inspiration, which at a few Birmingham crossroads mix commemoration and utility. Ornate high Victorian Gothic still arose in various parts of the city. Out in Aston, near Six Ways, a local architect named Arkell was responsible in 1886 for the violently late Gothic façade, with arches, oriels, gargoyles and grotesque beasts, of the Victoria Hall.

Another late work by Chamberlain was his incongruously Gothic extension of the Birmingham and Midland Institute; its niches, gables and pinnacles paid little respect to the Corinthian order and classical cornice of the older and neighbouring building. Chamberlain himself seems not to have cared for classical or Renaissance work for when, in October of 1883, he spoke at the institute on 'Exotic Art', he strongly sug-gested that architecture of this kind was exotic in England, adding hostile criticisms both of St Peter's, Dale End and of the Town Hall. Within an hour of the lecture he died, suddenly and without warning, aged only fifty-two.

The Italian palazzo was not quite extinct in Birmingham. In 1882, high up Cor-poration Street, the County Court building was finished as a restrained, two-storey palazzo, of quiet dignity and with its stone-facing a marked contrast to the colour of the building which soon arose as its very differently styled neighbour.

In 1890 Birmingham was the scene of a congress held by the National Association for the Advancement of Art. The congress itself was split into sections, and there were addresses from Alfred Gilbert, C. R. Ashbee, W. H. Bidlake, Aston Webb and other forward-looking artists and architects. The Fine Arts section had a specially interesting and entertaining speech from the well-known pioneer Arthur Mackmurdo, the founder of the Century Guild and an early British practitioner of Art Nouveau. His theme was the poor, over-ornate design standard found in most of the metalware made for the home or continental market, in many Birmingham workshops; he reinforced his point in what *The Builder* called a 'most piquant and practical manner'. He had, during his visit, gone to an establishment whose showrooms for local customers were filled 'with things no artist could endure'. But in the back rooms, where items could only be bought wholesale in consignments for distant export, he found and somehow obtained, two copper jugs of what he felt to be 'simple design and perfectly good taste'. These were for sale to negroes in countries where, by contrast with Birmingham's own suburbia, one found a 'half civilised coloured population'; the makers reckoned, for purposes of local sale, that these items which pleased Mackmurdo were 'not good enough for the reputation of the firm'. The lesson which the lecturer drew was that ornament was not necessarily art. Yet in Birmingham the time was soon coming when ornament of a lavish kind could be equated with fresh and forward-looking taste.

Before the meetings started, *The Builder,* whose editor Heathcoate Statham was sympathetic to the growing Arts and Crafts movement, gave ample space to the Birmingham congress, not least in a long critical article on architecture in the city. The article was searingly critical of what Birmingham's architects had lately achieved; its writer (perhaps Statham himself) made the point that what he felt to be the two or three good buildings of recent date were all the work of outsiders. He added the information that his paper had, for some years, hardly ever felt itself able to accept as illustrations any drawings sent in from Birmingham; among his more cutting judgements was the opinion that the Midland capital was 'one of the most architecturally depressing of all our large towns', and that its architecture was marred by 'a peculiar and defiant absence of beauty'. The new Council House he felt to be 'as poor and commonplace a piece of Renaissance architecture (of a sort) as ever gave employment to a competition draughtsman'; he was somewhat kinder to the façade of E. M. Barry's nearby Midland Institute. We can agree with his verdict on the profusely Renaissance Post Office which was finished, to Sir Henry Tanner's designs, in 1891, that it was both 'coarse and commonplace' and 'fussy and pretentious', while anyone who knew Corporation Street before its recent, none too pleasing modernisation will back the writer's 'quite painful' impression of the street when it was new. Anticipating Mackmurdo on the goods for local or African use, *The Builder*'s leader writer hazarded a guess that Birmingham's taste was influenced by its being a town of 'practical industries' which did not much consider beauty, and that there was, in the 'local bijouterie' a lack of refined and thoughtful work. Despite unstinted praise for one building then being finished, he could hardly have foreseen that in another seven years his paper would write on Birmingham's buildings in a wholly different vein.

The building whose example decisively influenced Birmingham's architecture was that of the Victoria Law Courts, originally meant for the site of the Council House extension, but actually placed near the top of Corporation Street. A competition for the complex of new buildings required was held in 1886, being won by Aston Webb and Ingress Bell. Their buildings, with a great hall which did obvious deference to Street's Law Courts in London, were finished in about four years; their style, their materials and their decoration came as a revelation to late Victorian Birmingham.

The Victoria Law Courts were in general a brilliant success. Their main failing lies in the harsh redness of the external terracotta, but compensation comes

in the creamy pink or yellowish brown terracotta of the delicately detailed interior. More remarkable, going far beyond the quantity of its earlier use in Birmingham, was the sheer extent of the terracotta employed as a detail and for complete surfaces. To the Corporation Street frontage, with its varied gables and windows at each end of the main hall block, the architect gave a spirelet above the louvre of the hall, and another spirelet to cap the northern tower. The style of the building, outside and in the superb interior of the hall, blends French flamboyant and English late Tudor; it was a clear, refreshing departure from the earlier English or Italianate Gothic long dominant in Birmingham. The French Gothic motifs arose from Aston Webb's enthusiasm, in this pre-classical phase of his career, for the rich detail of the period of François I. Inside and out, with its symbolic sculptured figures by Walter Crane the founder of the Art Workers' Guild, its richly coloured windows showing scenes in the city's history, and with the brilliant cusping and canopied work over its side entrances, the hall, along with the nearest parts of the Law Courts, make up a lavish building whose ornament *The Builder* found in some places to be somewhat too exuberant. In such features as the corridors, offices off the hall, and the doorways to the courtrooms it is, however, more restrained. But in its own time this 'entirely admirable' building was certainly 'far in advance of any other recent building in Birmingham'. Local architects were prompt to take the point.

Birmingham thus got confronted by an outburst of terracotta, excellent for the crisp, durable rendering of detail and used as never before. Its use went with a growing fondness for styles not, so far, as prominent in the Midlands as in the work, in or near London, of Norman Shaw and the architects who favoured the Renaissance styles and, for their Gothic, a Flemish rather than an English or Italian inspiration. The new fashion was soon well entrenched. It continued, in public houses and in small shops and offices, as well as in large commercial and corporation buildings, for another two decades. The local blend of brick and terracotta spread to churches, very often among the Nonconformists and in Anglican buildings by the local architect Thomas Proud. His church of St Aidan, Small Heath, is in fine, dignified Perpendicular, with its terracotta well restrained so that the pillars, arches, and window tracery resemble Midland sandstone. But in St Barnabas', Balsall Heath, the terracotta dressings are in a loud, unattractive pink.

In an issue of 1897 *The Builder* noted the obvious effect of The Law Courts on Birmingham's architecture, in the seven years since its earlier criticisms. Half a century previously, the city had used stone for its more important buildings. It was now 'tending to become a city of terracotta architecture'. The Law Courts had been the decisive new influence. Another writer spoke of 'the terracotta age', a contrast to the 'stone age' with its dignified Renaissance idioms, along Colmore Row.

Essex, Nichol & Goodman were among the first Birmingham architects to make a great, though not an exclusive use of terracotta; they expressed it in continental late Gothic or Flemish Renaissance style. Their splendid late Gothic façade of the Technical School in Suffolk Street was of about 1893. They later worked on fantastic flamboyant Gothic designs, whose buildings no longer stand, for shopping and commercial façades in High Street and a site close to that of the Old Square. Elsewhere their terracotta ornamentation was in the Flemish–Jacobean Renaissance taste. This was specially true of the new meat market and slaughter house whose foundation stone was laid in 1895; it is conspicuous for its tall tower and corner turrets, for its plaques of

rams' heads and skulls and of bullocks' heads, and for the attractively rounded
at its north-eastern corner. A building which combined a workmen's club and
offices and a savings bank was another Essex, Nichol & Goodman work in a
Renaissance vein, but with some details more akin to those of the Arts and C
movement. The brothers Ewan and James Harper, who did much work for
Birmingham Methodists, designed their late Gothic Central Hall (opposite the L.
Courts) with a slender spired tower whose graceful lines rise finely at the top
Corporation Street. Not far away, in the YMCA headquarters in Dale End, they produced an imposing façade in a richly varied Flemish Renaissance idiom. Bateman &
Bateman also worked both on lavish terracotta and on the simpler housing favoured by
the Arts and Crafts movement. Two of their commercial buildings, planned about
1900 but never built, would have been pioneers in their structural use of concrete
and steel. William Henman's wide-spreading buildings for the new general hospital
were another important achievement, early in the 1890s, in the use of terracotta with a
Flemish Renaissance style. Another partnership which charmingly used terracotta with
an emphasis on Flemish Renaissance or a somewhat simpler Jacobean style, was that
of T. W. F. Newton & Cheatle. Their work appears well in offices and professional
chambers on the Colmore estate, while the ingenious charm of Newton's Renaissance
and baroque detail on the frontage of the City Arcade in Union Street shows that
his death, in 1903 aged only forty, was a sad loss to Birmingham's architecture.

The Martin & Chamberlain office, from 1883 under William Martin who later took
his son Frederick as a partner, very naturally continued to exploit the terracotta fashion
which Chamberlain and Martin had largely initiated. Their masterpiece, at the corner
of Edmund and New Hall streets, was the Telephone Building dated 1896, somewhat
unhappy in the precise redness of its terracotta, but an exciting work, inventive in
much of its decoration, and with foliate carving, in the roundels and gables above
some of its arches, akin to that which Chamberlain had placed in the wheel window
of his School of Arts and Crafts.

Martin & Chamberlain's output of board schools, still with varied, imaginative
spired towers, went on till the end of last century. By then William Martin was dead,
and some people in authority felt that the firm (which had designed pumping
stations and lunatic asylums, as well as schools) had too large a share of the municipal
work, so in 1902 H. J. Buckland succeeded the younger Martin as the school board's
architect. Martin & Chamberlain had also worked with distinction on some public
libraries. Their Gothic work in brick and terracotta was bold and imaginative, particularly in the clock towers which, like the spires of the firm's schools, rose appealingly
above drab surroundings; in those days when few people had portable clocks or
watches, clock towers were, in their several districts, a prized amenity. Other architects designed some of the city's many new libraries. Like the Martin library in Small
Heath these were sometimes conjoined, in a specially local endeavour to cater for
corpus sanum along with mens sana, with public baths. Cossins & Peacock, who in
1891 had designed the Nechells Green Library with its domed Renaissance clock
tower and symbolic terracotta sculptures in its window heads, were responsible, in
1895–6, for the Jacobean-Renaissance library whose whimsically capped clock tower
adorns Moseley Road; the Gothico-Renaissance baths, with a pair of turrets and
yellowish-brown terracotta, were added some ten years later by William Hale.

The normal, stone-faced Edwardian baroque also became fairly common in central

Birmingham, and in small outlying buildings. In Steelhouse Lane the Harpers' tall, imposing block for the Wesleyan & General Insurance Company was predictably Flemish in feeling and detail; it was finished, like Arthur Harrison's inventively baroque Digbeth Institute, in 1907. Philip Chatwin, who worked much for Lloyd's Bank, designed its handsome Ionic branch at Five Ways, also the imposing New Street building which combines Ionic and Roman Doric. A simpler classical treatment, with shallow Ionic pilasters used along with some sensitive brickwork, was given, in 1913–15, by S. N. Cooke to the Repertory Theatre, on its constricted site in Station Street and with its gallery rising in a phenomenal steepness.

The classical styles were little favoured among the religious bodies. The one exception to the normal Gothic or increasingly Romanesque pattern was the new Oratory church, built between 1903 and 1909 and designed by the normally Gothicist Doran Webb of Salisbury, a kinsman of Sir Aston Webb. The style of the domed, basilican church is that of the Renaissance as this was known in Milan or Rome fairly early in the sixteenth century; the choice was that of the Oratorian fathers who required a church whose feeling was that of the time of St Philip Neri their founder. The marble-lined sanctuary, the space beneath the dome, and the splendid, monolithic Corinthian columns which support the nave's tunnel vault are the best features of a building full of beauty and character.

The insurance companies were now very active in the baroque taste. In 1907 the London & Lancashire, architecturally enterprising in Birmingham and elsewhere, saw the completion of their New Street building with its dome, its ornate portal, and much decoration by Bidlake's Birmingham Guild of Handicrafts. In Colmore Row, Paul Waterhouse, like his father well entrenched in the insurance world, was another 'outsider' who designed a Birmingham building. His modest-sized office for the Atlas Assurance is an interesting morsel of Edwardian baroque, in tune with some other buildings in the same street but not with the small office, not far away and for the Eagle Insurance Company which W. R. Lethaby had designed in 1898. Though some of its lower details are within the simpler Gothic or Renaissance conventions, its plain upper storeys, unstylistic and topped by a blank stage where a chequerboard pattern of brick and stone is varied by plain stone roundels, came as an innovation by a prophet of the Arts and Crafts movement which soon gave Birmingham some restrained and sensitive buildings.

With the work of its Arts and Crafts architects Birmingham came into the forefront of England's building achievement. This applied to churches, to buildings for various public uses and to houses, whether individual buildings for wealthy owners or grouped in the model or garden suburbs for which the city is specially famed.

The leading figure among the architects who, between the 1890s and the outbreak of World War I, served Birmingham so well, was William Henry Bidlake. He was mainly though not, in his domestic work, exclusively a Gothicist. His Gothic work displays the influence of Bodley (under whom he had studied) and his own sensitivity. His churches, in an improving contrast with most of Birmingham's Victorian places of worship, looked more to English late fourteenth-century Gothic than to the earlier Gothic which had fired the ecclesiologists. They were, however, given inventive touches of Bidlake's own. St Agatha's, Sparkbrook, much damaged inside by a fire in recent years, but with its almost East Anglian tower strikingly dominant over the Stratford Road, and the nobly composed tower and eastern apse of the Bishop

35

Latimer church in Handsworth, are Bidlake's finest ecclesiastical works. Another of his good churches, started earlier than these two, is St Oswald's, Small Heath, strongly under Bodley's influence, looking back to a somewhat earlier Gothic style, and with a foliate spandrel which resembles Martin and Chamberlain foliage, or even Art Nouveau which Bidlake came to dislike. The vicarage, dated 1899, deserts Gothic for a charmingly simple Queen Anne idiom, decked out with some patterns favoured by Arts and Crafts enthusiasts. St Andrew's, Handsworth, started in 1907 is, however, more in the Decorated manner of about 1340.

The Arts and Crafts movement found fine domestic expression, in the hands of Bidlake, C. L. Ball, C. E. Bateman, and other architects, in houses built in leafy suburbs by prosperous Birmingham citizens. Some critics, among them some of *Country Life*'s contributors, had by the last Edwardian years come to hold views on central Birmingham's architecture less favourable than those which had hailed the Law Courts and their terracotta progeny. A writer in 1910 felt that the centre of the city was 'hardly an architecural paradise'; for him the 'unhappy influence' of the Law Courts was only slightly offset by the 'quiet character' of Leonard Stokes' Telephone Office and of some other recent public buildings. But the suburbs were a different story. There, under the influence of Lethaby and others, one found a close-knit, characterful school of local domestic architects, well exploiting the 'peculiarly hard and sound' local brick, almost the only available material for the main structure of buildings in an essentially brick country. The Tudor or Jacobean style, simply expressed in late Gothic or Renaissance forms, was common in these quietly tasteful Arts and Crafts houses whose idiom had been pioneered elsewhere by such architects as Voysey or Lutyens. One also found the style, more extensively and with even more restraint, in the unassuming excellence of houses in Birmingham's model or garden suburbs.

When in 1879 the Cadburys first moved to the semi-rural setting of Bournville, their new factory, by a local architect named George Gadd, was a low, sprawling building of no distinction; a few houses, in a normally and nastily mid-Victorian polychrome Gothic, were also built for a few key workers who had to live on the site. Later factory extensions, with a crop of little cupolas in the Arts and Crafts taste, were by G. H. Lewin of the firm's estate office. The same architect designed the first of the company's welfare buildings, the girl employees' baths of 1902–4 whose ornamental foliage was decidedly Art Nouveau and whose clock tower, with its fancifully supported cupola and dome, was a notable, non-municipal addition to this class of Birmingham's buildings. By now the separate enterprise of the Bournville village, at first financed by Cadbury money but never a part of the actual firm, was well under way.

The Cadburys, with Quaker reforming zeal, had long been interested in model industrial housing. Once the Bournville factory had got established they turned to the creation of a spaciously laid out garden suburb where trees and grass verges lined the numerous roads, and where each house had its own garden. The first houses were put up in 1895, the Bournville Village Trust was formed in 1900, and by 1904 over 500 houses had been finished. A few public buildings, built simultaneously with the estate's earlier houses, were grouped near the central green. Among them were the school with its sturdy, oriel-windowed late Gothic tower, the faintly Tudor Quakers' Meeting House with its polygonal corner turret, and the Arts and Crafts Jacobean cultural centre of Ruskin Hall. More remarkable in some ways, and much more numerous, are the houses with their sober brickwork, some pebble-dashed or half-timbered walls,

36

a few gently curved 'eyebrows' over first-floor windows, and a striking variety of chimney designs. Here, within ten years of its commencement, was a pioneering, quickly famous garden suburb. The architect was William Alexander Harvey, a pupil of Bidlake whose Birmingham houses gained him more than local fame. The German critic Muthesius admired his work and illustrated one of his Birmingham house interiors in his important work of 1904–5 on English houses. We hear, moreover, that in some European countries Harvey was reckoned as one of Britain's leading architects.

Bournville was not the only Birmingham district where garden suburb architecture now arose. The Harborne estate was founded in 1907 by John Sutton Nettlefold of the firm of Guest, Keen & Nettlefold which had, however, no connection with this further venture in progressive housing. Martin & Martin were the architects for the estate, less spaciously laid out and less leafy than at Bournville, but compactly and attractively centred on the Circle, with its Arts and Crafts social hall in the middle plot and some pleasant houses like those in the adjacent roads. Many of the estate's houses, as one sees them in North Gate and High Brow, are paired or in sets of four, while in Margaret Grove the end house of one quartet has plaques with the date 1908 and the letters H.T. for Harborne Tenants. Out at Ward End some similar ideas were employed a few years later in the Sutton Trust estate, a small garden suburb whose houses, by E. C. P. Monson, have some tile hanging and much attractive Arts and Crafts detail. As the inscription on a Roman Doric pillar explains, it was built (as were similarly conceived estates in other towns) under the will of William Richard Sutton, a London carrier who died in 1900. It was finished in 1916.

Garden suburbs were not, however, the whole of Birmingham's late Victorian or Edwardian housing. Builders who knew little of garden city planning or the artistry of Arts and Crafts still covered large tracks of land with continuous rows of small houses which had tunnel alleyways, small back yards, and even tinier front plots. So in Bowyer Road in Saltley, Arden Villas are dated 1894 but are in the Gothic taste of the 1870s. At Erdington the houses in Holliday and Hart Roads, built in 1906, had Victorian Gothic window heads filled with carved flowers and foliage of the type which Martin & Chamberlain pioneered before 1883.

Birmingham's greatest Edwardian building project lay somewhat apart from what was generally being done in this period of terracotta and Arts and Crafts. Mason College, since 1896 a university college, blossomed out in 1900 as a fully chartered university. Joseph Chamberlain was its first Chancellor, and new buildings were soon started on the Edgbaston site. The University Council held no competition but went straight to Aston Webb & Ingress Bell. This annoyed some of the project's subscribers, also the local architects who wanted a competition in which they and others would have their chance. The chancellor was asked, apparently without result, to receive a deputation, but early in 1902 the Webb & Bell designs were approved, and by the start of 1903 work was well in hand. The university's plan, with its radiating blocks in a way recalling the layout of prisons arranged for the use of the panopticon, was unusual for any academic grouping; a semicircular design was, one gathers, suggested by the natural contours of the site. It allowed for seven radiating blocks, with two more, along the diameter, which would directly adjoin a great central campanile. This semi-circular group of buildings would only fill a small part of the spacious suburban site, and the tower was to rise directly at the end of an avenue of trees running in from Pritchatt's Road; this avenue's interruption, and its partial obliteration, by recent buildings was a sad casualty of the university's modern growth. For their main buildings the architects achieved more spectacular effects. In the imposing vestibule of the Great Hall, with Ionic marble columns and an upper rotunda below its dome, unmixed neo-classicism appeared. In the actual hall, with galleries and cross arches giving it a kinship with Aston Webb's almost contemporary assembly hall (or quarter deck) in the Royal Naval College at Dartmouth, debased Gothic was used in the window tracery, likewise in the windows of the other blocks whose ornamental ends impressively surround the courtyard and make one regret that an empty gap, where one block should have been built, was left in the curved sequence. But the university's external impression, with its striking series of saucer domes, was less Gothic or Renaissance than Byzantine. In particular, the hall block seems like some great Byzantine basilica and the slender campanile, in fact a separate building and closely modelled on the fourteenth-century Torre del Mangia at Siena, was first designed in a more Byzantine manner nearer to that of the exciting new campanile of Bentley's Westminster Cathedral which was nearly finished when Birmingham University's designs were being drawn, and whose row of saucer domes may also have given Webb and Bell (the latter of whom was Bentley's close friend) some ideas for the unusual silhouette of the academic grouping which Edward VII opened in 1909.

INTER-WAR

Though World War I brought many changes to Britain it did not, in Birmingham or elsewhere, lead to any marked shifts in aesthetic taste or architectural style. In the first few post-Armistice years the main urge was for a return to the known securities of late Edwardianism, for a continued use of period styles, and for the continuance, less relevant as time went on, of such idioms as baroque, neo-Jacobean or the studied, increasingly self-conscious simplicities of Arts and Crafts. In factories, however, and in commercial buildings by such architects as Marcus O. Type who had flourished before 1914, Birmingham's industrial zones saw the growing use of such modern constructional devices as frameworks of steel or reinforced concrete. But for many of these buildings the veneer remained 'period', or else included well patterned external brickwork like that of the pre-war Arts and Crafts designers. Terracotta, however, declined as an external finish, leaving the fine brickwork of Midland building practice more firmly entrenched. Several architects such as Harvey and Bidlake, who had been busy in Birmingham before the war, remained there after the Armistice, while late Victorian or Edwardian names, such as Cossins and Essex, still appeared.

The first few post-war years thus saw a continuance, in Birmingham's central business area and elsewhere in the city, of pompous Edwardian baroque; some of the designs may have been made before 1914. One found the style, with a mixture of Tuscan half-columns, fasces and key pattern decoration, in the exterior of the Phoenix Insurance Offices and in the Hall of Memory which was put up, as a forerunner of more ambitious civic developments, in the reasonably uncumbered ground at the eastern end of Broad Street. A competition was held for what was bound to be a prominent, aesthetically important addition to Birmingham's architecture. S. N. Cooke and W. N. Twist were the winners, and theirs was the design which took shape. The dim interior of this domed octagon, with its Roman Doric aedicules and porch, is more impressive than what one sees outside. The whole building was of modest size and neither vulgar nor pretentious as were some other contemporary war memorials. If less of our own century than some of the monuments simultaneously put up in Germany, it was not on that account, and in the 'period' aesthetic climate of England in the 1920s, to be despised. Less excusable, despite the classical precedent set by the memorial hall, are the somewhat later, Ionic neo-classical buildings of the Municipal Bank and Baskerville House, designed in the 1930s by Cecil Howitt of Nottingham. Both of them, at such a time and in one of the great cities of Europe, were stylistic anachronisms. The marble and craftsmen's works in the hall of Baskerville House remind us of a time when building costs allowed lavishness and artistry.

Neo-Georgian, along with mock Tudor and imitation Jacobean, also appeared in some of the large suburban public houses which are a marked feature of Birmingham's outskirts. The idea behind these much subdivided drinking palaces was that the multiplicity of their bars would suit them for family drinking as distinct from an almost wholly male patronage. At Northfield C. E. Bateman's Black Horse, an amazing long-clerestoried blend of stone and half-timbering, with twisted chimney stacks, carved barge boards, gables and oriels, is one such hotel in the black and white West Midland vein of about 1500. The Fox and Goose at Washwood Heath is similar, but with its infilling and tall chimney stacks in brick. The pseudo-Jacobean inns, some of them by Holland Hobbiss who now came to the fore, are on the whole more tasteful and satisfying, while those in the Georgian idiom exude a feeling of steady sobriety shared by the banks, baths and libraries which were now built in this currently favoured taste. The breweries which owned public houses in the area also had a policy whereby many older, unattractive inns were replaced by new, more socially acceptable buildings. The Bear, and the Antelope, on the Stratford Road, both by Holland Hobbiss in a pseudo-Jacobean style, were good examples of an attractive trend.

The period was not, in Birmingham, a time of outstanding factory architecture. At Longbridge the Austin works continued their important, stylistically unimpressive growth. In Bournville Cadbury's new factory blocks, and a works dining hall of about 1928, were by a Glasgow architect named James Miller and contained Georgian brick and stone references less remarkable than such fashions had been in the early days of the Bournville Village. The estates of the Bournville Village Trust continued to grow. Some areas, like Weoley Hill and some land close to the Bristol Road, had first been colonised before 1914, and the whole expanded garden suburb now had its influence on some of the corporation's new housing estates, and on districts like King's Heath and Hall Green where privately built housing, more varied in its designs and less obviously controlled than in Bournville, shows how an example had been set by Birmingham's pioneers of seemly suburbanism. In the city's dingier areas some courts and tunnel-back rows of houses were pulled down, and a start was made with municipal blocks of flats. Those off Garrison Lane in Bordesley, built between 1927 and 1929 by D. H. Davies the City Engineer's Housing Architect, were given polygonal-headed doorways, gabled compositions above those doorways, tiled mansard roofs, and delicately patterned brickwork which made them more interesting, as architecture, than other blocks of flats put up in Birmingham before 1939 or since World War II.

Most of Birmingham's Anglican and Catholic churches built between the wars abandoned the Gothic style; Byzantine and Romanesque, rendered in excellent brickwork with a minimum of stone, were favoured. The trend had, indeed, been set before the war. Arthur Dixon, an architect and silversmith of the Arts and Crafts school who had worked sensitively on at least one simple frontage in Great Charles Street, was the designer of the striking little church of St Basil in Deritend, started in 1910 with attractive patterned brickwork in its façade and a mosaic in its apse. St Germain's in Edgbaston, whose preliminary competition attracted Dixon, Bidlake and some other important local architects was the work, between 1915 and 1917, of Edwin Reynolds who also produced good patterned brickwork in the manner of Bentley at Westminster, along with simple Romanesque arcades inside. The same architect was responsible about 1930, for the large, narrow-aisled and clerestoried basilica of St Mary at Pype Hayes. Even Harvey adopted basilican-Romanesque in his parish church at Bournville, while in the 1920s, the basilican Catholic church at Sparkhill, by E. B. Norris who was asked to make a study of Rome's Byzantine churches, was given a medievalist Roman campanile. Another Roman campanile, later than the actual church, adjoined Harrison & Cox's Catholic church in Aston. For a cruciform emphasis, again in a Catholic church, one can turn to Saltley where the imposing building by G. H. Drysdale was finished in 1934. Its sturdy, simple central tower, the good detail of its transepts, and its apse with mosaics and a semi-polygonal baldachino on four Corinthian columns, make it of considerable note. Not far away, in Alum Rock Road, Holland Hobbiss worked typically of himself in the simple basilican design, western porch and quiet brickwork of St Mary and St John's Anglican church which was started in 1934.

Though he had been trained in London, Holland Hobbiss, a Birmingham man by birth, was a friend and associate of Bidlake, Harvey and other local architects of the Arts and Crafts school. Their influence, and his own preference, led him to an adherence to the period tradition which was linked, appropriately in a West Midland architect, to a love of fine brickwork and a deep understanding of its use. So one finds, in Mr Hobbiss' Birmingham work, a most craftsmanlike use of brick, particularly in his educational buildings. At Saltley College, where his father had taught, he designed a residential block, and a charming Principal's Lodge in a simple domestic Queen Anne manner; both of them proved him a delicate worker in variously coloured brick. At the university his Students' Union, dated 1930, astonishingly recreates the style, the elaborate chimney stacks, and the red brickwork with a criss-cross diaper of blue, of a late Tudor manor house in East Anglia. Across the road, never deliberately grouped with the Union but well complementing it, his new buildings for King Edward VI's School have more attractive diapering in the brickwork of the lodges and of the governors' block. The main buildings—with a Big School whose oriel window and other architectural features have a Jacobean Gothic flavour, and whose hammerbeam roof recalls that of Barry's Big School in New Street and includes some of its timbers—form another carefully rendered period essay, started in 1937 and unfinished when war broke out. Beyond the main group a brick-faced, rectangular chapel lovingly enshrines the Perpendicular stonework of Barry's upper corridor on the school's earlier site.

All this period work of the 1930s was beautifully done. It may have seemed backward-looking, but it was not untypical of a time when truly modern architecture, in Birmingham as in some other provincial cities, was largely lacking. Modernity, in a somewhat bulky and dominating manifestation of yellowish grey brick and lighter coloured stone, first made its appearance in the medical and teaching blocks, and in the commanding tower of Lancaster & Lodge's first buildings of the Queen Elizabeth Hospital, now dated in comparison with the vast quantity of architecture which has burst on Birmingham in the last twenty years.

POST-WAR

In Birmingham, as in some other towns, post-war building started slowly except in the housing field. It was well into the 1950s before people saw the great avalanche of architecture which has made many of those who live and work in the now declining city centre, and in some less central districts, feel that they must endlessly endure the dust, the reddish mud, the clatter and the road diversions of a building site. Civil engineers, contractors, and architects have combined, with patchy results, to give Birmingham more new buildings and more new highways, than in any similar past period; the central area has largely become a town of this century. In the centre, and in such districts as Ladywood and Newtown, the builders of today have slaughtered the Victorian town as ruthlessly as their Victorian predecessors destroyed the considerable fabric of Georgian Birmingham. Nor is the process at an end; any final section which records the city's finished projects must needs seem somewhat incomplete. The new City Library, with a part of the inner ringway running directly below it, and the towering Independent Television Building near the beginning of Broad Street, are soon sure to be visually significant additions to the central townscape.

After some essential repairs to bomb-damaged buildings, and with some progress on schools and houses, the opening post-war phase was comparatively tame. The garden suburb pattern continued, under the Bournville Village Trust at Shenley Fields and elsewhere, and under the Corporation whose houses in the area of Weoley Castle stood on land bought from the Trust and had to conform to the neo-Georgian or Arts and Crafts standards already ruling for their dwellings. Churches still hankered, with restraint, for basilican planning, while the restrictions of those years allowed no public buildings of any note. Housing, in the first few years from 1950, was a main preoccupation; from about 1955 the current onrush got into its stride. The offices of the City Engineer, Surveyor, and Planning Officer, and of the City Architect, have been specially active in the city's reshaping; but much building work, serving many purposes and of varying, often considerable merit, has been designed by architects in private practice. Most of them are local men who have, except in the University, had most of the Birmingham commissions.

What central Birmingham and the inner suburbs have lately experienced is a three-fold cataclysm. Many streets in the well known central district have been so heavily rebuilt that they present the appearance of virtually new highways. Corporation Street, High Street and Dale End serve to demonstrate the point. Some well known buildings have been wholly renewed, and familiar landmarks have nearly or entirely disappeared. The Market, the whole area of the Bull Ring and New Street station typify the trend, while the Repertory Theatre of Sir Barry Jackson and S. N. Cooke is due for demolition on the opening of its successor off Broad Street. All but a fraction of the Great Western's famous station at Snow Hill has been obliterated, while the opulent Victorian Renaissance Grand Hotel has gone the way of the station's forebuilding to open up a combined site for more angular and functional development.

The second aspect of Birmingham's steel and concrete revolution is the creation round the old centre of an inner ring road. By such a device Birmingham has made a kind of visual truce with the needs of the motor car which is so leading a source of the city's prosperity. The road, with its complex system of intersections, flyovers and underpasses, links up with such old highways as the Hagley and Bristol Roads, or with a set of new expressways, streaking out on their stilts or in cuttings, across the inner suburbs, and making it easy for the heavy traffic of modern Birmingham to speed out from the centre towards the trunk roads and motorways of the Midlands. At intervals along the ring road pedestrians are helped by subways, and by sunken enclosures whose coloured mosaics, vividly commemorating such facets of the town's history as the Civil War, the ancient horse fair, and (best of all) the Great Western Railway, are among the better features of a dramatic, still unfinished surrender of a traditional city centre to some aspects of modernity.

With new office blocks and stores in its centre and in the areas of Broad Street and eastern Edgbaston; with its suburban shopping precincts, and with its churches, schools, and many new buildings for industry and the public services, Birmingham claims, perhaps with good reason, that it has become a city of this century, and that it now contains more buildings of our own time than any other city in Britain, or perhaps in Europe. For some years now it has certainly been a building contractor's paradise. The class of building which has, above all others, given substance to its claim is housing —in the public and private sector, in separate houses, low-rise groupings, and in clusters of rows of point blocks containing privately or publicly owned flats.

Birmingham's recent housing achievement has not merely lain in the repair of war damage, nor in the rebuilding of houses and the building of new flats along previously existing lines of streets. New road projects would alone have frustrated such two-dimensional conservatism. Planning has, however, been carried much further. In whole districts which once were densely built over with streets of workshops and continuous rows of two-storey houses, the earlier road pattern has been erased; for many such areas no town map is now useful if it is more than five years old. This process of clearance, and of drastic replacement, was well seen in Nechells Green (an early example), in Lee Bank, in the low-lying area of the Rea Valley between Bristol Road and Balsall Heath, and on one side of Bath Row and Holloway Head. The road here drops steeply to the two great thirty-two storey blocks of the Sentinels, newly built and towering in an assertive dominance over the inner ring road, and the shops, restaurants and new Albany Hotel of Smallbrook Ringway. The same drastic refashioning has occurred in Ladywood, in once elegant Newtown, and at Erdington where a fine sequence of tower blocks is well screened by the undisturbed trees which still grace one side of Sutton Road. The point blocks themselves tend to be standardised and rectangular, gaining more, as in the Stevenson Tower near New Street Station, in the great block which rises challengingly above the underpass at Six Ways, and in the row along the site of the Crescent, from their siting and landscaping than from any high intrinsic beauty. But they are very much a part of Birmingham today. Nor is modern housing confined to municipal work. The Bournville Village Trust has added considerably to its total of dwellings, and private enterprise housing has proliferated considerably. On the Calthorpe Estate in Edgbaston tall blocks like West Point, new patches of attractive low-rise houses, and the infilling with new houses of what were once the gardens of large villas, have diversified a suburb which has, in the process, lost some character but little of its leafy beauty.

The central area naturally contains many of the more individually important new buildings. They tend to be lofty, bulky and angular, with their architects using steel or concrete frames, and in their structure being exponents, with various cladding material, of the 'international contemporary' style which leaves little room for great variety between towns, or for much basic variation, except in the grouping of component masses, among any one city's more important buildings. The varieties of style, or the individual, purpose-revealing decoration, of Birmingham's Victorian buildings, are a thing of the past, and though many of the city's large new blocks are fine works of their own time, well exploiting the scenic qualities of their sites, some of them could as well be in other cities. Of those whose planning and silhouettes are basically rectangular, one of the finest is the extremely up to date office and production building of the *Birmingham Post and Mail,* by J. H. D. Madin of the John Madin Design Group whose offices in Hagley Road are themselves in one of their more distinguished business blocks and who have now come forward as one of the city's chief architectural partnerships. Their newspaper block is remarkable for the relationship achieved between its spread-out lower storeys with the spacious, delicately coloured entrance hall, and the tower block which seems lightly poised on the lower element and whose cladding of dark grey glass gives much distinction to one of the city's best-known, far-seen modern buildings. The most familiar exception to the rectangular trend, and the modern building by which, above all others, one now knows Birmingham, is the Rotunda by James Roberts, whose prospect-commanding office is on one of its topmost floors, and which climbs high above one end of New Street, the market area and the reconstructed station. The building's basic shape is that of a great cylinder well set off by the gently curved walls and vertical windows of the building which envelopes its base. The concrete panels of its cladding are made luminous by their mosaic coating of white glass.

Much less happy are the two nearby modern features—the Bull Ring covered shopping centre and New Street station which now, after its almost complete rebuilding, takes nearly all Birmingham's railway traffic. The Bull Ring Centre has a sad, confusing, unattractive interior. Its planning, by Sidney Greenwood and T. J. Hirst, is ingenious, and the notion of so comprehensive a shopping place with an adjacent bus station and many-tiered car park, tunes in with modern ways of movement and circulation. But the cavernous interior, from which egress always seems difficult, is less helpfully thought out than such a covered precinct should be. Considerably better, with its fine clerestoried shopping hall and its other piazzas, is the new shopping centre recently laid out by Cotton & Ballard above the unhappily unattractive New Street station. British Rail's replacement of the older building has, no doubt, its working advantages to counterbalance the loss of the dingy, but characterful earlier station, once distinguished for its great single-span roof and unusual for the public path which intersected it and gave ticketless access to the platforms below. In the new complex the platforms are featureless, draughty and comfortless, more like the platforms of an underground station though without the colourful diversion of their posters. The inner concourse has a functional, businesslike appeal, but the wider, noisier space of the outer concourse is a disaster, much uglier than the equally space-consuming, none too attractive entrance hall of New Street's opposite number at Euston. As one sees it from its forecourt, the station's outward aspect is slabby and uninviting, a sad contrast to the welcoming, backward-sloping grace of the great entrance canopy at Roma Termini. The transformation of the station was finished late in the 1960s, a creditable job when one remembers that it had all the time to stay in use.

Some other secular buildings in Birmingham present a happier picture. The most conspicuous is the Post Office Tower, now the highest building in the city and impressively simple in its plan, square with its corners cut back for most of its slender height, but with its concrete structure ending, below a set of circular galleries for its dish aerials, in a simple square. Down in the lower part of Edgbaston the new Broadcasting House in Pebble Mill Lane is nearly complete, a complex building by the Madin Group with a clean, horizontal emphasis for the glass and concrete tiers of its principal block. On a smaller scale the same designers' forebuilding for the much older Alexandra Theatre is an admirably modern contrast, with its vertical members and great expanses of glass, to the less distinguished work behind it. Along Hagley Road a building of some character, in an area now notable for fine blocks of offices, is the Automobile Association's building whose designers, Harry Bloomer & Son (also the architects of a large new factory in Hockley, with pleasant panels of green slate, for Samuel's the large jewellery firm), have put a multangular, polygonal entrance hall in front of a fairly ordinary rectangular office block. The same favoured area has lately seen, amid its late Georgian or Victorian houses, the rise of many new office blocks. The offices of Tube Investments, from the 1950s and before the more 'contemporary' phase of such architecture in Birmingham, are neo-Georgian in style but not in the all important matter of scale. Far better, with a contrast between the mainly horizontal impression of its less lofty block and the strong vertical effect of the mullions in its taller element, is the Chamber of Commerce Building by the Madin Group, at the corner of Harborne and Highfield Roads. Back at Five Ways the scene is now dominated, above a new shopping piazza, by the tall Auchinleck House designed by the Seymour Harris Partnership; its narrow end tapers slightly towards the crossroads, in an irregular half polygon, and two blank wall spaces are well varied by the colours of great abstract murals in mosaic and glass. Pedestrian shopping piazzas and precincts, of various sizes and with their buildings of differing heights, are now agreeably common in Edgbaston and in several outer suburbs such as King's Norton, Erdington and King's Heath, providing car-free havens for leisured shopping.

The jewellery quarter already has a few post-war buildings, while flatted factories, in modern blocks, are replacing some of the cramped but characterful workshops which here, as also in the gunsmiths' streets, lurk behind late Georgian or Victorian façades. Industrial commissions have figured largely in the work of Birmingham's architects, small practices being engaged on them as well as the larger groups. Cadbury's architectural department did well on the office block of 1966, with its bowed end wall towards the road, which rises in contrasting modernity between the Arts and Crafts half-timbered ranges and the more ambitious clock tower of the women's baths. At King's Norton the rectangular office tower which the Triplex Safety Glass Company have put up within their works is by James Roberts, and ranks, with its clean lines and outer surfaces of aluminium and black glass, as one of Birmingham's best office blocks. Further out, and stretching a little way over the border with Worcestershire, the Austin Works at Longbridge, now an element in British Leyland's industrial empire, have lately seen much change and growth. The earliest post-war buildings, among them the first of the new car assembly buildings, were by Howard Crane, an architect from the United States who died in 1952; his successors are the Birmingham practice of Harry Weedon & Partners who have worked elsewhere for British Leyland, and who have designed a school and some blocks of flats for the Birmingham Corporation. The best of their new buildings at Longbridge are round the large, airy quadrangle laid out on the artificially levelled site of an upland airfield. The reception

44

and administrative buildings, with a boldly rounded entrance at the junction of two rectangular blocks, stand on the northern side of the court; a little beyond it a striking circular building with large spaces of glass and a low clerestory capped by a shallow dome, was first the showroom for commercial vehicles and is now a styling studio. The main drawing and design office, built in 1961-2, has clerestory lighting and, thanks to the design of its steel frame, a notably helpful spaciousness. In the upper sector of the works the canteen has nicely varied brickwork, while the most monumental building on the site is the eight-tiered car park.

Other important new buildings relate to the city's health and cleanliness. The Lancaster & Lodge practice, which designed the new Queen Elizabeth Hospital in the 1930s has added, in a more starkly contemporary style, to the large cluster of buildings; they are also the architects of a new maternity hospital in Edgbaston. Down towards Castle Bromwich the new refuse disposal works by the City Architect's Department, with the structure of the buildings of smooth, easily cleaned reinforced concrete, are of both architectural and technical interest.

Many churches, for the worship and other activities of various faiths, have been built in the last few years. Some, like the unconventionally roofed Welsh Presbyterian chapel, by James Roberts in the shadow of one of the Sentinels, are in central districts, but more are in outer suburbs or in newly settled zones. A large mosque is also projected for the slum-cleared tract at one extremity of Balsall Heath.

Though the clients and the architects of Birmingham's earlier post-war churches mostly deserted the period styles, they still favoured the rectangular, basilican planning which had been normal before 1939 and which also appeared in the new Coventry Cathedral. Though the shape of these buildings was, in the eyes of modern liturgical pundits, outdated, this did not mean that the churches themselves were bad architecture. Some new churches, among them the Methodist chapel at Sparkhill which was started in 1959, the Methodist church at Northfield, and the Catholic church of Christ the King in Kingstanding, were given simply designed towers at one corner of their main buildings. In the garden suburb setting of Weoley Castle the Catholic church by Adrian Gilbert Scott has a scenically placed western tower, with a fine elliptically shaped outer arch answering to a sanctuary arch, of similar shape, at the top end of a long clerestoried nave. The local architects Bromilow, While, & Smeeton (the designers of Sparkhill Methodist church) also worked for the Anglicans in new housing areas at Longbridge and Quinton, on the rectangular pattern. Traditional styles and traditional church planning, could, however, continue into the 1960s. One sees it in the long, narrow Catholic church in Yardley Wood, finished as late as 1966, with Romanesque details and a sturdy, pyramid-capped tower above its sanctuary. More astonishing, and a strange exotic in the garden suburbia not far off the Bristol Road, the Serbian Orthodox Church is one of Birmingham's architectural surprises. By a Yugoslav architect, Dr Dragomir Tadic, it was carried out by the architectural department of the Bournville Village Trust which also designed the unashamedly contemporary house for the priest. But the church itself, for a religious body which seems to have heard little of contemporary architecture or liturgical change, is wholly in the Byzantine tradition as this flourished in fourteenth-century Serbia. It is of brick with dressings and details of stone, transeptal and with a western turret as well as the invariable main dome of an Orthodox church. Its bronze doors and candelabrum were made in Yugoslavia in the Byzantine manner. Its worshipping space has no seats and ends in the *eikonostasis* and the enclosed, apsidal sanctuary of Orthodox practice. The frescoes in bright, assertive colours, derive closely from Serbian medieval paintings.

Churches planned on lines which had, for many centuries been unusual, have also in the last few years made frequent appearance in Birmingham. Pioneering religious buildings are no surprise in a city which has, by the work of the university's Institute for the Study of Worship and Religious Architecture, become an important, sometimes controversial centre of modern liturgical thinking. Central or 'auditory' planning has sometimes, as in the Catholic church at King's Heath where a Greek cross plan goes with a simple Byzantine style, been rendered in period dress. Normally the structure, materials, style, and decoration are more committedly of our own time.

Of the new Anglican churches, St Matthew's at Perry Beeches, by Robert Maguire and Keith Murray, finished in 1964, was hailed, and has had its influence, as a church whose main worshipping space is an irregular hexagon, and where the main masses of the structure ascend in an angular, somewhat graceless helical pattern. The interior, despite a dauntingly ugly cliff of brick and concrete behind the altar, is imposing in a sheer if graceless severity. At Hodge Hill what can be reckoned as a religious and social complex has caused great interest, and some dislike, for the way in which its main worshipping space and some of its social facilities are architecturally united and visually linked. In the upland housing area of Bartley Green the new church, less innovating in some respects and by a London architect, Mr H. Haines, is square-planned with a high pyramidal roof; it has among its furnishings some sculpture by Mr John Poole, a Midland artist whose work has added much distinction to a banking hall in the Rotunda and to some other buildings in Birmingham.

The Nonconformists too have been active, and at Highgate the Baptists' church cum social centre, by Professor Denys Hinton, has its lounge and recreation room even more closely united than at Hodge Hill with a rectangular, simply furnished worshipping space. Professor Hinton has also designed a new Congregational church on a square plan with shallow polygonal recesses. It has attractive vertical windows at its corners and some interestingly irregular silhouettes. This church has now replaced the late Georgian and Victorian building on the historic site at Carr's Lane.

Nor have the Catholics been behindhand in providing for their large congregations. The new church of St Catherine of Siena, replacing the Hansom-Cossins building which fell to the inward swathe of the southern approach to the inner ringway, is circular (though its laity do not worship all round the main altar), with a pleasingly simple, clean-cut campanile which does Harrison & Cox the architects more credit than the ponderous, somewhat gasometer-like main structure. Much more inspiring, with varying but always striking structures and with good fittings—including some excellent modern glass and, in one at King's Heath, an outstanding pierced metal figure of Christ by John Poole—are the three new churches at King's Heath, Tile Cross and Sheldon, the first by Mr J. Edmundson of Desmond Williams & Associates whose main base is in Manchester, the other two being fine 'contemporary' essays by Mr Robert Brandt of Sir Giles Scott, Son & Partner. In the King's Heath church the helical design, in a mixture of concrete and yellowish brick, rises in a smoothly curving sweep towards the base of the slender brick tower with its simple cross. At Tile Cross, a splendidly finished, finely decorated church, with the Stations of the Cross in mosaic, is on the plan of a stumpy-limbed T, and three sides of its worshipping space are enveloped, as if by folds of drapery falling in the angular pattern of a con-

46

certina, by gracefully curved expanses of concrete roof. Concrete, with some plum-coloured brick, is the main material of St Thomas More's at Sheldon where the ground plan is a severely compressed pentagon, and where the brickwork and striking glass of the sanctuary have above them a challenging twin 'spire' whose two main elements enclose a cross; an effective end to its approach from the busy Coventry Road.

Lastly one can glance at new buildings which, in a city whose concern lies more and more with things not narrowly confined to its commerce and industry, serve the purposes of culture and education. Those of the Cannon Hill Arts Centre, set on the riverward edge of a charming park, are attractive and, on their modest scale, appropriate for their task. One awaits with eager curiosity, the finishing of the new Repertory Theatre. Many new schools have arisen, and new school buildings, better suited to modern needs, have replaced some of those designed by Chamberlain and Martin. In the Ada Road School in Bordesley the caretaker's lodge, the gabled tower, and the slim timber spire survive as mid-Victorian relics amid a modern educational grouping. Teacher training is cared for in the buildings by the City Architect, a mixture of a lofty block and lower elevations, in Westbourne Road amid the villas of Edgbaston. More important, and for some years likely to stay in such a position, are the new buildings of the two universities now within the city.

The University of Aston, originally the College of Advanced Technology, had a dispiriting start when it found itself housed in what had been the Central Technical College, put up after 1945 but to pre-war designs for a bulky, uninspired block which combined the modernity of the 1930s with neo-Georgian backward glances. It is hard to think of a university whose original main building is more soulless than this one whose more fully neo-Georgian neighbour, of the same pre-war decade, is the main fire station. It may also be the only English university whose principal block is capped by a wireless mast. Later buildings, among them the Students' Union and a building which contains the affiliated architectural department, are more thoroughly of the 1960s. But the feeling of an academic precinct is lacking. This is now being provided in the nearby area which still (in 1970) contained Gem Street, the modern Kyrle Hall and Birmingham's first groups of municipal housing. A campus of a more promising type is being laid out, with its buildings designed by Robert Matthew, Johnson-Marshall & Partners whose buildings at York and Bath have given them practice in modern academic architecture.

In the older, much expanded University of Birmingham the architectural position is different and much more advanced. Once post-war expansion started there was some infilling on the original, radial site, and a reminiscently neo-Georgian Mechanical Engineering block was started, soon after 1950, by the local architects Peacock & Bewlay. Mr Verner Rees, a London architect, then got out a comprehensive scheme for completing the campus within the bounds set by Pritchatt's Road. It was neatly thought out, compact, but a little unimaginative. Its main building was to be the Library, facing out towards the Chamberlain tower, across a newly created second court and dominated behind by a tall tower. From 1957 onwards the Library was built, without its tower but with a fine stairway giving it a monumental approach. To one side, and in part flanking the second court, the unexciting but competent Arts Building is another part of the Verner Rees scheme. Since then, however, the University's architectural policy has changed. What almost amounts to an academic *Hansa-viertel* has been created, with Casson, Conder & Partners as its general supervisors

47

and with many notable architects asked to show their paces. So Birmingham University has, as it were, a display gallery of contemporary English architecture. The high-rising, impressive quadrangle which houses botany, biology and other kindred subjects is by Playne & Lacey. Such well known London partnerships as Casson & Conder themselves, Chamberlain, Powell & Bon, Howell, Killick, Partridge & Amis, and Arup Associates have designed buildings of varied size, grouping, materials, and quality. But the effect is less good than one might expect from the abilities of those who have taken part. The effect is cramped and overcrowded as well as lacking in the stylistic unity of the University's earlier schemes. This applies, in particular, to the area towards the canal whose ornamental qualities could, if kept from the attentions of the local highway engineers, give the University of Birmingham a charming waterside pleasance. Beyond Pritchatt's Lane, and up among the beautifully sited, spaciously disposed modern halls of residence the position is easier, and one feels less acutely, among the University's more northerly buildings, that the campus has been allowed to get overcrowded. The most imposing of the new buildings, straddling University Road as the new City Library will squat over a length of the inner ring road, is the Arts and Commerce tower, an honest though somewhat brutal building by Arup Associates. Its two blocks, arranged *en echelon* like the same architects' main elements of the Leckhampton Graduate Hostel for Corpus Christi College at Cambridge, are joined by a linking section which on one side clearly reveals its function as a staircase tower also containing the lifts, and on the other side holds lavatories and the cleaners' rooms. The Drama Department has its studio theatre in the podium, there is one large lecture theatre, and the two main blocks hold the usual assortment of lecture rooms, offices, common rooms, and seminar rooms. From the second court, past the Library and the earlier Arts Building, the new concrete and glass composition is impressively entered by a concrete stairway which lends an almost baroque touch to this area of great significance for the new architecture of Birmingham.

A Short Booklist

Bird, Vivian. *Portrait of Birmingham* (1970)
The Bournville Village Trust, 1900–1955 (1955)
Chatwin, Philip B. *Life and Story of J. A. Chatwin* (1952)
Dent, R. K. *The Making of Birmingham* (1894); *Old and New Birmingham* (1880)
Dugdale, Sir William. *Antiquities of Warwickshire*, vol II (2nd edn 1730)
Gill, Conrad, and Briggs, Asa. *History of Birmingham*, 2 vols (1952)
Hickman, Douglas. *Birmingham* (1970)
Hutton, T. W. *King Edward VI School* (1952)
Hutton, William. *History of Birmingham* (1780)
Langford, J. A. *A Century [1741–1841] of Birmingham Life*, 2 vols (1868)
Pevsner, Nikolaus, and Wedgwood, Alexandra. *Warwickshire* (1966)
Shaw, R. Stebbing. *History and Antiquities of Staffordshire*, vol II, part I (1801)
Smith, William. *A new and Compendious History of the County of Warwick* (1830)
Victoria County History of Warwickshire, vol VII (1964)
Victoria County History of Worcestershire, vol III (1913)

1 Aston Old Church, tower and spire; fifteenth century.

2 Northfield Church, chancel; thirteenth century.

3 The Old Crown, Deritend; late medieval.

4 Stratford House, Bordesley; late Elizabethan.

5 Aston Hall; Jacobean Renaissance.

6 The Great Drawing Room at Aston Hall may first have been the Summer Parlour. It is, perhaps, the finest and certainly the most opulent room in the mansion. Its chimneypiece, somewhat belatedly, displayed German or Flemish Renaissance idioms rather than Italian classicism, and the strapwork ceiling was almost outdated at the time of its erection. In the frieze, the figures in the niches are some of the Nine Worthies —Old Testament characters, prominent Christian heroes, and 'honest pagans' whose representation was popular when Aston Hall was built. The mullioned and transomed windows of the room still looked back to an older building tradition.

THE CATHEDRAL

7 Archer's Baroque: the baroque character of Archer's fine church of St Philip is specially clear from its exterior. The domed tower, and the window below it with its massive segmental pediment, make an imposing western composition. The concave sides recall those of Wren's tower at St Vedast's church in London.

8 Borromini in Birmingham: the influence of the brilliant baroque architect Francesco Borromini, whose work Archer had seen in Rome, is specially marked in the pilasters and pediments of the corner doorways at St Philip's.

9 The old Cross of 1703, and the Welch Cross of 1706.

10 From this and other pictures, it is clear that the Old Square was an attractive formal grouping in vernacular baroque.

THE NORTH PROSPECT OF Yͤ SQUARE IN BIRMINGHAM

11 In Temple Row: this attractive baroque doorway, with its 'swan's neck' pediment, must have been installed soon after 1719 when Temple Row was started. It survived till a few years ago but has now, unfortunately, been destroyed.

12 In Moor Street: the building which was once Dingley's Hotel has now been pulled down. It was another good example of late baroque by local craftsmen; its giant pilasters resembled those in Old Square.

13 King Edward VI School. The three-sided, brick and stone buildings in the local baroque manner were built in 1731-2.

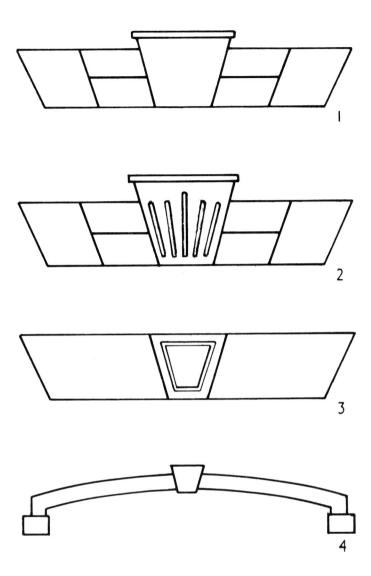

14 BIRMINGHAM WINDOW HEADS, c 1740–1800.
In cream-painted stone against dark red brick:
  1 Moor Street, Holloway Head, and elsewhere
  2 Cannon Street and elsewhere
  3 Temple Row, New Meeting Street
  4 Lozells Road, Ashted Row, Woodcock Street, etc

15 (*opposite*) The Monument, or Perrott's Folly, 1758.

16 This house in Great Brook Street, now destroyed but at first standing in a district of some elegance, well showed the late eighteenth-century idiom, with slender Roman Doric pillarets subdividing its windows, which Birmingham builders used for many houses of the better type.

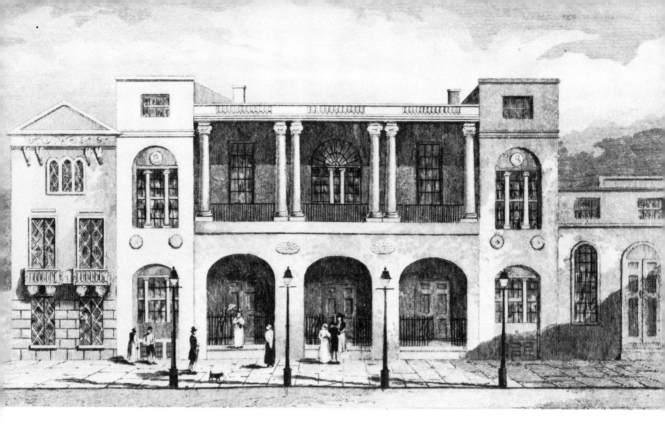

17 and 18 Samuel Wyatt's elegant and well balanced façade for the theatre in New Street (*above*) was designed in 1777 and finished in three years. The Crescent (*below*), had it been completed as planned in 1788 by John Rawsthorne, would have been among England's finest late Georgian urban compositions.

19 St Mary's Chapel, by Joseph Pickford in 1774, was notable for its octagonal nave and its Gibbsian steeple.

20 and 21 The balanced buildings of the once rural Soho Factory (*above*), and of the Canal Office (*below*), were among the best Georgian buildings serving the early phase of Birmingham's industrial and transport revolutions.

22 Chantrey's fine seated statue of James Watt is dated 1825 and was set up in a chapel which Rickman added to Handsworth Old Church. A drawing of a steam engine is engraved on the inventor's scroll.

23 Nelson's statue, with its vigorous bronze figure backed by a draped anchor and by the bows of a warship of the great admiral's time, is surrounded by railings in the form of naval boarding pikes. By Richard Westmacott and set up in 1809, it is early, and most admirable, among England's many Nelson memorials.

24 The Public Offices were built, for the magistrates and the Street Commissioners, under Birmingham's third Improvement Act, passed in 1801; the building also included some prison cells. The classical block, with Ionic half-columns, was designed by William Hollins and was his most important work. It was started in 1806 and finished the following year. Some important alterations were made by Charles Edge whose drawings, including a fine elevation, a new rear block, and a good dome to light the main staircase, are in the Edge Collection in the City Library.

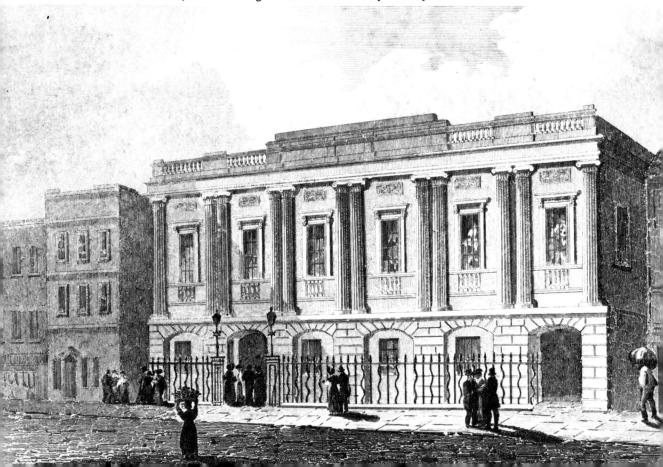

25 Birmingham's canal marina has an attractive row of restored boatmen's cottages across its western, or upper, end. It lies in a delightfully rejuvenated section of the plentifully locked waterway which links the Birmingham and the Birmingham & Fazeley canals.

26 The old crane on one bank of the canal marina fits well into the scene but was brought from elsewhere.

27 and 28 Lee Bridge (*above*) of 1826, spans Telford's direct, deep-set cut which shortened the course of the Birmingham Canal. The attractive iron bridge (*below*) of 1827 is one of many which formed part of the same great feat of waterway improvement.

29 The Gun Barrel Proof House, with its brick range dated 1813 and with a splendid, highly appropriate coloured trophy of arms, is purpose-built from the days of the Napoleonic War and the Industrial Revolution. Its uniqueness and beauty make it of much more than local importance. A Deritend builder, John Horton, designed it, and the sculpture was by William Hollins.

30 This factory front in Granville Street is of the nineteenth century, but its façade is still in the plain, unadorned late Georgian tradition; the windows have iron glazing-bars.

RAILWAY MASTERPIECE

31 and 32 The Ionic Curzon Street terminus of the London to Birmingham railway was designed by Philip Hardwick (the architect of the Doric propylaeum at Euston) and was finished by the end of 1838. It was soon superseded by the more centrally placed New Street, but fortunately survives as a goods station. Along with Brunel's Tudor Gothic terminus at Bristol it is one of the supreme memorials of the early railway age. The arms of London and Birmingham fittingly crown its entrance doorway.

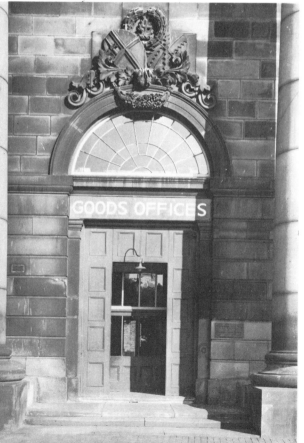

GOODS OFFICES

33 and 34 Waterloo Street (*above*), an 'improvement' completed by 1830, shows various aspects of the Greek Revival. In this picture, No 35 has an Ionic porch and plasterwork of this artistic movement's richest phase; the next-door house displays Egyptian influences. The bank (*below*), by Rickman and on the corner with Bennett's Hill, is a fine Corinthian building of 1830.

35 and 36 (*opposite*) The Society of Artists' portico (*above*), of 1829 and by Rickman, and a fine villa in Calthorpe Road (*below*) well show other characteristics of the Greek Revival.

THE TOWN HALL

37 By Joseph Hansom and started in 1832, the Town Hall at Birmingham is England's best example of the Roman temple form applied to a leading public building. The Corinthian porticos and side colonnades have all the authority of pure classical architecture. The open arcade, by which one enters the building, is due to the gently sloping site; it is not the least effective part of a justly famous building.

38 Christ Church, up its flight of entrance steps, imposingly filled the still existing triangular site between the top of New Street and the western end of Colmore Row. With the Gibbsian inspiration of its portico and tower it was designed by Charles Norton and finished by 1814. Though the scene was now urban the accompanying architecture was still in a minor key. Since then the townscape has changed immensely, and none of the buildings shown in this charming print still stand. The church was destroyed in 1899; the bodies in its vaults, including that of Baskerville the great printer, were reburied in the cemetery at Warstone Lane. The buildings which replaced the church have themselves been pulled down in the last two years.

39 Charles Edge's drawings for the Greek Doric chapel in the Key Hill Cemetery are in the collection in the City Library. The chapel, resembling others of the same type in other towns, was built in 1834 and recently demolished.

40 Carr's Lane Chapel is interesting both in the Congregational story and for its architectural history. Whitwell's imposingly fronted building of 1819-20 succeeded earlier chapels of 1748 and 1802

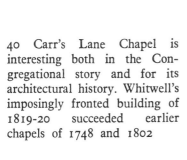

RICKMAN CONTRASTS

41 and 42 The Bishop Ryder Memorial Church (*above*), demolished a few years ago, stood in Gem Street on a site now part of the area being developed as the campus of Aston University. It showed Rickman in his Gothic vein, and was one of the architect's last works. St Thomas', (*below*), an earlier church, was started in 1826 when Bishop Ryder of Lichfield and Coventry laid the foundation stone of what was then a chapel in St Martin's parish. The gracefully contrived western feature is among Rickman and Hutchinson's best Grecian achievements.

43 Set behind a Doric portico in Graham Street, the Mount Zion Chapel was built in 1823, and for most of the time before its demolition was used by the Baptists. This rare photograph shows its fine interior, in shape recalling the famous Octagon Methodist Chapel at Taunton, and a good example of an ' auditory ' worshipping space.

EDUCATIONAL TUDOR

44 and 45 Simultaneously under construction in the 1830s were Barry's new block for King Edward VI School (*above*) and Potter's three-sided quadrangle at New Oscott (*below*). Both effectively used the Tudor Gothic common in the ancient universities, and much favoured in the nineteenth century for scholastic buildings.

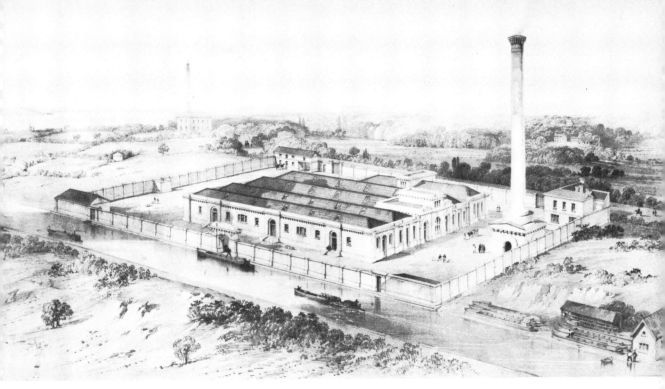

46 The canalside lead works, by William Herbert of London in 1837, were spaciously laid out on an unencumbered site. The Italianate style gave monumental character to buildings of a type previously treated more simply.

47 The dignified style of this early Victorian factory front in the jewellery quarter comes between the severity of those built in the 'Regency' tradition and the ornate Italianate or Gothic effects lavishly employed by the mid-Victorian factory architects.

48 and 49 Charles Edge's design of 1836 for a simply composed Greco-Italianate bank in Union Street (*above*) is one of several for business premises in the Edge Collection. His charming design for a fluted pedestal letter box (*below*), with its vertical slit, is of 1855.

VIEW NEXT CAUSWAY

POST OFFICE

50 The new prison at Winson Green was started in 1844 on a site, near the old course of the Birmingham Canal, bought by the Gaol Committee of the newly constituted borough. It was finished in 1849, with separate cells for male and female criminals, for debtors, and for younger offenders. Its cells, in buildings behind the castellated entrance then thought suitable for prisons, numbered 321. Its architect was D. R. Hill who also designed a municipal asylum and some public baths, and who hoped to become the borough's permanent architect.

VICTORIAN MINIATURES
51 and 52 The lodge of a large Edgbaston garden (*above*) and a fountain in Gosta Green (*below*) are amusing Gothic buildings in a minor key. The latter contrasts quaintly with its modern background of Aston University's Students' Union.

53 and 54 The BSA Works at Small Heath (*above*) by T. W. Goodman in 1862, and the somewhat later Argent Works (*below*) in the jewellery quarter well displayed Birmingham industry's mid-Victorian use of round-arched, polychrome Italianate styles.

55 and 56 The Great Hampton Street Works (*above*) dated 1872, were designed by an architect still unknown. They were built, for Green & Cadbury's who made pearl buttons, by a Mr Cadbury who may have been a relative of the chocolate family.

They well show the use of High Victorian Gothic on an industrial façade. In Granville Street (*below*) the plaque, on a factory once engaged in making saddlers' ironmongery, is one of several which show the characterful, very local use of sculpture to denote a trade carried on in a building.

57 J. A. Chatwin's sketch of his still existing bank (now Lloyd's) in Temple Row West charmingly records the arrival, in the 1860s, of a tall Renaissance *palazzo* into what was still a basically Regency scene.

59 (*left*) J. A. Chatwin's dignified tower and spire at St
Augustine's, Rotton Park, finely
sited at the end of an approach
road, were added in 1876 to a
church of the previous decade.
60 (*below*) St Alban's, Bordesley, a great apsidal church by
J. L. Pearson, mainly dates from
1879–81 and is of brick and
stone. It is the most stately
Victorian church in Birmingham
and has always been a High
Church stronghold.

58 (*opposite*) The central features of the Council
House by Yeoville Thomason are dated 1878.
The pediment sculpture shows Britannia crown-
ing Birmingham's manufacturers with triumphal
laurel wreaths; the world at large rewarded them
more highly.

61 In this late Victorian photograph the Chamberlain Memorial Fountain is seen against the elaborately composed front of Mason College, opened in the previous year.

STEEPLED SCHOOLS

62 and 63 The William Cowper Street School (*above*), in what is now the Newtown redevelopment area, was built soon after J. H. Chamberlain's death and may be from his designs. The school in Tilton Road, Bordcslcy (*below*), is of 1891, from the time when the Chamberlain & Martin practice was run by William Martin.

THEOLOGICAL GOTHIC

64 and 65 The ornately designed, centrally towered Congregational Spring Hill College (*above*) of 1854–6, by Joseph James, may have had some influence on Ball & Goddard's Handsworth College (*below*), opened in 1881 for the Methodists.

66 Joseph Chamberlain's Moseley home, Highbury, designed by his namesake J. H. Chamberlain and built in 1879–80, is among Birmingham's historic houses. It was built before its owner became really famous in national politics, at the peak of Joseph Chamberlain's municipal career.

67 Edmund Street contrasts. On the right a High Victorian Gothic commercial building has continuous arcading all along its top storey. On the left, a brick and terracotta frontage, dated 1897 and with Beaux Arts and Arts and Crafts detail, has plaques with the initials CJE.

68 The Victoria Law Courts, by Aston Webb and Ingress Bell, completed in 1890, came as a brilliant revelation of the possibilities of terracotta used on a monumental scale. The creamy-pink entrance hall, with Flemish Gothic idioms and some French Renaissance detail, makes a splendid introduction to the rest of the building.

69 The novel trellised and foliate filling of the round window at the College of Arts and Crafts in Margaret Street was one of J. H. Chamberlain's last designs.

70 The brilliance of the detail in the Great Hall of the Law Courts is well
shown in one of its two identical entrance archways.

71 (*opposite*) The Flemish Renaissance style of Ewan and J. A. Harper's YMCA building, of 1900–4, gave Birmingham another spectacular terracotta façade.
72 (*above*) Bright red terracotta and original detail combined in William Martin's
telephone building, dated 1896.
73 (*below*) The original court of the University, with its semicircular plan and domes
in the Byzantine manner.

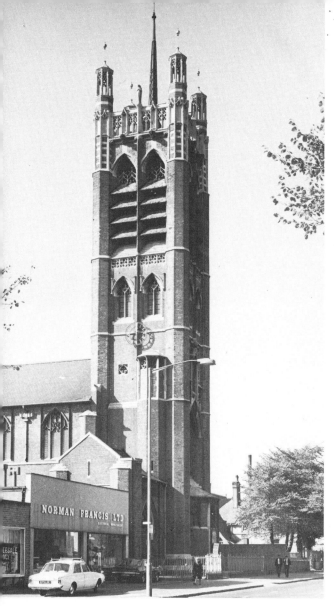

74 Dominant over a section of Stratford Road, Bidlake's splendid Arts and Crafts Gothic tower at St Agatha's is the finest feature of the church built in 1899–1901. Decorated tracery blends with a somewhat East Anglian impression and a 'Hertfordshire spike'.

75 Bidlake's Bishop Latimer church at Handsworth is of 1903. The east end, with its carefully composed apse, shows various Arts and Crafts Gothic motifs, and the tower loses no effect from being unpinnacled.

76 Of the public libraries designed by the Chamberlain & Martin office in William Martin's time, the one with the most graceful exterior is that at the bottom of Spring Hill, dated 1891 and finished in 1893. The interior has heavy red marble columns, Gothic arches, a gallery, and an arched ceiling.

77 Less conventionally Gothic than the Spring Hill library, William Martin's library at Small Heath dramatically occupies a triangular site which also includes public baths. It was opened late in 1893.

78 One of Chamberlain & Martin's best buildings for the Birmingham Waterworks was the Pumping Station at Longbridge, in deep red brick and terracotta, impressively composed but smaller than its photograph suggests.

79 Arts and Crafts Renaissance design is well seen, at Bournville, in Cadbury's baths for girl employees, by G. H. Lewin and built in 1902–4.

80 and 81 The Bournville Village Schools (*above*), with a later cupola for the carillon now capping the tower, and the Quakers' Meeting House (*below*) are two of W. A. Harvey's important public buildings near the village centre. The turret of the Meeting House adds a romantic touch to its design, while figures in the Renaissance taste grace the school's Gothic oriel.

ARTS AND CRAFTS HOUSING

82 and 83 The engagingly pierced chimney stacks of a house in Bournville (*above*) show one of Harvey's many interesting and inventive chimney designs. At Harborne (*below*) a row of maisonettes by Martin & Martin has its doorways ingeniously reached at two levels.

84 In the Oratory, of 1903–9, the monolith marble columns, the barrel vault, the dome and the apsidal sanctuary are important features of Doran Webb's fine Renaissance church.

85, 86 and 87 On Moseley Road (*above left*) the library (*right*) and the public baths (*left*) well show Birmingham's use, around 1900, of a Jacobean Renaissance style rendered in brick and yellow terracotta; (*above right*). In Deritend a faithfully Roman campanile, much like that of S Giorgio in Velabro which was Newman's titular church, is among Birmingham's architectural curios. Its small basilican church was built, privately as the chapel of a hostel for working boys, by Fr John Lopes, an Anglo-Catholic clergyman who in 1915, before his building was finished, joined the Church of Rome. The church was never used for services, and has always served secular purposes; (*below*) in the jewellery quarter the iron clock-tower was erected by Joseph Chamberlain's constituents to commemorate his conciliatory visit to South Africa soon after the Boer War.

88 and 89 The Hall of Memory (*above*), with bronze figures outside and a quietly solemn interior, is Birmingham's best known inter-war Renaissance building; (*below*) the flats off Garrison Lane, of 1927–9, are of much character for the design of their projections and the delicate variety of their brickwork.

90 and 91 The varied period styles and sensitive brickwork of Holland Hobbiss are contrasted in the University Union (*above*), dated 1930, and in the Tennis Court Inn at Perry Bar (*below*), finished in 1939.

92 The *Birmingham Post and Mail* building, by the John Madin Design Group, is well known for its silhouette, for its dark grey cladding, and for its far-seen, minute by minute record of the time of day.

93 and 94 (*this page*) Auchinleck House (*above*), by the J. Seymour Harris Partnership, presents a canted end to the busy crossroads and underpass at Five Ways. The striking abstract murals are by Trewin Copplestone. Commercial Union House (*below*), another office block by the Seymour Harris Partnership, has cladding of Carrara marble and runs lengthways to Corporation Street.

95, 96 and 97 (*opposite page*) The John Madin Design Group are the architects of the block (*above left*), running back from Hagley Road with its mellow exterior brickwork, which houses their own offices. The banking hall low down in the Rotunda (*above right*) is notable for its abstract mural, in *ciment fondu*, by John Poole. James Roberts' gently curved terrace of shops and offices along Smallbrook Ringway (*below*) is of historic interest in that it was the first set of buildings completed along the new Inner Ring Road.

98 and 99 The Priory Road (*above*) and Metchley Grange (*below*) Corporation housing areas combine high and low rise buildings and attractive landscaping. Both won Ministry of Housing awards.

100 Of the mosaics on aspects of Birmingham history the most vivid, fittingly near the remnant of Snow Hill station, is that which recalls the city's connections with the GWR; this section deals with the years 1909–20.

101 The AA Offices in Hagley Road, with their bold polygonal forebuilding, are by Harry Bloomer & Son.

102 and 103 Recent buildings in the Austin works are by Harry Weedon & Partners. The circular one (*above*) was originally the commercial vehicle showroom, and the multideck park (*below*) is for vehicles awaiting dispatch.

104, 105 and 106 Sparkhill Methodist church (*above left*), with its copper-topped tower, was started in 1959; its architects were Bromilow, While & Smeeton. The Serbian Orthodox church (*above right*) at Bournville is something of an exotic in modern Birmingham. John Poole's pierced metal figure of Christ dominates the semi-circular worshipping space of the new Catholic church at King's Heath (*below*).

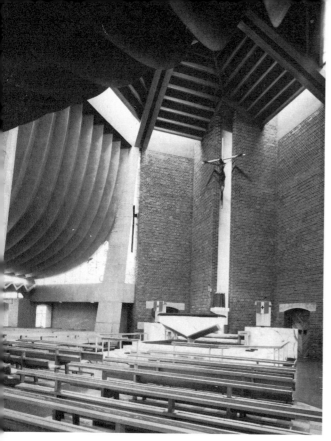

107 and 108 Two of Birmingham's new Catholic churches are by the now 'contemporary' partnership of Sir Giles Scott's successors. That at Tile Cross (*above*), smaller than it seems from photographs, is remarkable for a dignified sanctuary, the concrete 'folds' of its roof, and for John Chrestien's windows. At Sheldon (*below*) too the church has Chrestien windows, but is also noteworthy, from outside, for the concrete main structure and steeple of its nave.

109 The new Carr's Lane Congregational church, by Professor Denys Hinton, is a modern successor to more conventionally rectangular chapels.

110 In the new ecclesiastical and social complex at Hodge Hill, emphasis is laid on the weekday use of the main worshipping space for socially helpful secular activities.

UNIVERSITY OF BIRMINGHAM

111 and 112 The Commerce Building (*above*), by Howell, Killick, Partridge & Amis, has a striking polygonal interior hard to include in a single view. Dignity and a monumental feeling are expressed in this view of Arup Associates' Arts Tower (*below*).

Topographical Gazetteer

An exhaustive architectural gazetteer of so large and varied a city as Birmingham would need to draw on the meticulous wanderings of a lifelong, expert resident. I have known the city for nearly forty years, increasingly well in the last three, but I cannot claim, despite many sightings and researches, that this survey is complete. It does, however, cover much ground, and it may contain points which others have missed. Not much appears, in the central region, on buildings covered in my introductory section. I have almost confined my attention to buildings complete at the time of writing, and I have, from personal preference and because of the great local significance of the period between 1890 and 1914, given special treatment to Georgian buildings and to terracotta and Arts and Crafts.

Region 1

Certain points in the central area within the river Rea, Five Ways, Ladywood, Icknield Street, Lozells Road and Nechells Place down to Saltley Viaduct.

The cathedral remains one of the best buildings in this area. Temple Row has changed much since 1719, but two brick-faced, early Georgian houses survive. A late Victorian baroque building has a charming corner spirelet, while at the corner of Waterloo Street an office block has a fine late Gothic terracotta façade.

New Street has changed many times. Its best recent building, with overhanging top storeys, is that containing, shops, offices and the Conservative Club designed by Harry Bloomer & Son. Above the station, the new shopping parade is more orderly than the Bull Ring Centre. Period styles appear in the red terracotta, Flemish Gothic-cum-Renaissance Arden Hotel (of 1896 and later), in Philip Chatwin's Edwardian baroque Lloyd's Bank, and in Holmes' fine Midland Bank palazzo (see page 27) with its rich coved, panelled and coffered ceiling. Other period buildings include a Flemish Renaissance block in dark terracotta by Essex, Nichol & Goodman, which once housed the Art Nouveau splendours of the sadly lost Kardomah Café. The London & Lancashire Insurance building, finished in 1907 and by Riley & Smith, is Edwardian baroque, domed and with a portal, with décor by Dixon's Handicrafts Guild.

The lower end of Corporation Street is unrecognisable to those who have only known it as a Victorian highway, but opposite the Law Courts the slim, square tower of Ewan and James Harper's Methodist Central Hall (1903) still beckons with the turrets, late Gothic windows, and engaging lantern of its ornamental top. The grand stairway and the hall are disappointing, but the exterior has charming corner turrets, historic and symbolic sculpture, and much Renaissance detail.

Arts and Crafts buildings are excellent in the streets of the Colmore estate. Among the clifflike modernity of recent office blocks, Edmund Street has, in Nos 125-7, an Arts and Crafts Jacobean façade; on No 133 are William and Mary touches of 1898. Cornwall Street, largely Flemish Renaissance, has some excellent busi-

ness chambers of the 1890s. Nos 93 and 95 are by Newton & Cheatle, while Rodway & Co's premises, dated 1913, have a plain façade with giant arches and diamond patterns in their spandrels The lower section of Great Charles Street has good Arts and Crafts or Edwardian classical façades; that of Rodway, Drew & Hopwood, with giant arches, is masterly in a harmony of tiling, brick and stone. Church Street has attractive Newton & Cheatle work and neo-Renaissance fronts.

Vast demolitions, and rebuilding with standardised council flats have changed much of Ladywood, wiping out in a healthful transformation, the old pattern of streets. King Edward's Road still has a late Victorian factory whose corner turret features rosettes in its window heads and, at its top, a far-seen, truncated cone.

Despite demolitions, the jewellery quarter still blends late Georgian houses and workshops (notably in Caroline Street and Warstone Parade) with Victorian industrial façades (see plates 47, 54 and 55). A heavy, classically inspired façade occurs in Northampton Street, while a fine vertical emphasis, with good Arts and Crafts brickwork of 1913, distinguishes the West Parade Works. Down in Icknield Street, near Edge's heavy Grecian entrance piers at Key Hill Cemetery, the Mint has a good mid-Victorian Renaissance frontage.

Beyond Bridge Street, and its two severe Lucas factories, Newtown's western reaches are another zone of massive rebuilding. Lozells Road is an architectural mess, but some characterful buildings lurk south of it. The library of Lozells Methodist church was started by Crouch & Butler in 1893; it has a Romanesque façade, quaint corner turrets, and gates of good art metalwork. In Berner's Street, St Peter's Mission by Arkell (started in 1899) has a whimsical Perpendicular frontage, while a simple Italianate façade graces Lozells Congregational church.

Towards Saltley Viaduct a raised expressway traverses a changing factory area. Nechells Green, with clustered blocks of flats more appealing than their rectangular successors, saw Birmingham's first great post-war clearance and new building. It still has the red brick Gothic church of St Matthew, pre-ecclesiological and of 1839-40. The library, started in 1891, was by Cossins & Peacock. Its terracotta sculpture includes such edifying subjects as Industry, Crafts, and Learning, and a dome caps its good Renaissance clock tower. A modern religious building is the Catholic church of St Vincent de Paul, by Louis Hayes of S. N. Cooke & Partners, opened in 1968. The Hardman studios have made the windows of the polygonal baptistry and the outdoor mosaic of St Vincent's life, which are the church's best decoration. Not far away, a small estate of inter-war, pseudo-Georgian housing is arranged as a series of the locally favoured courts. The White Tower, a public house dated 1932, is a jazzy period piece.

Region 2

Old Aston and part of Witton; Gravelly Hill, Erdington and towards Pype Hayes.

Aston Cross is graced by a cast-iron Ionic column supporting a double-lamp post, and by the clock tower designed with a Romanesque emphasis by Arthur Edwards; it was cast in Glasgow. In 1891 Lewis Spokes Richards gave it to the Aston Local Board.

This district is dominated by the bulk and odours of Ansell's brewery and the HP Sauce factory. Its appearance has changed with demolition, new housing and the concrete stilts and roadway of the Aston Expressway. Along Park Road is Aston Hall (see pages 8-9) and Aston's original parish church. Each aisle still has medieval masonry, refaced when the church was rebuilt and enlarged eastwards by J. A. Chatwin. The dignified nave combines Victorian Decorated and Perpendicular; the apsidal chancel, recalling St Michael's, Coventry, is imitation Perpendicular. The church's glory lies in its tombs and monuments. That of Sir Thomas de Erdington and his wife, shows outstanding alabaster work; that of Sir Thomas Holte, commemorates the builder of Aston Hall; the mural to Sir John Bridgeman (d 1710) put up in 1726, was designed by Gibbs.

North-west of Aston church the undistinguished stands of Villa Park football ground are prominent. Trinity Road leads west, past latish Victorian housing in such thoroughfares as Jardine and Emscote Roads, where effect is produced (as elsewhere in Birmingham's inner suburbia) by shallow, squared or polygonal bow windows. Some pavements are set in attractive patterns of blue brick, while the imposingly wide Broadway has ornately foliate doorway and first-floor window heads. All Souls', Witton, of 1907 and by Philip Chatwin, is cruciform with a simple, square Perpendicular central tower. It has, like St Peter's, Handsworth, by J. A. Chatwin, an Arts and Crafts Gothic feeling.

Further east towards Six Ways, Arden Road has a spectacular Victorian display of paired Gothic arches, pointed doorways, foliate arch heads and elaborately gabled porches. Mansfield Road Methodist church, with a striking Decorated façade and a wheel window in a retaining arch, is of 1883. Christ Church Baptist church is a fantastic polychrome exercise by James Cranston, of 1862-5, and with brickwork mixing red, yellowish white and blue. The body of the church, with iron internal pillars, has rounded octofoil windows; it is joined by a strange arcaded vestibule to a tower whose stone spire, supported by ornately tabernacled pinnacles, has a flavour of St Mary's spire in its architect's city of Oxford. For the adjacent Victoria Hall see page 31. In Witton Road the Albert Rooms, belatedly named in 1899, have a fairly simple Renaissance façade in terracotta. Lower down, is the Library by Alexander & Henman. Its corner tower has a baroque cap; the rest, with some pleasing Arts and Crafts railings, is restrained brick and terracotta neo-Jacobean. Down Witton Road a Catholic church of 1922 and by Harrison & Cox, is in the Italian Romanesque then favoured by local Catholics. Mosaics, *opus sectile*, and marble panels complete its Byzantine impression; the brickwork of its Roman campanile is of the 1930s.

Between Aston and the bottom of Gravelly Hill is the unlovely sprawl of the GEC works at Witton. Some trim Regency villas look down on the bewildering jumble of the road complex which connects the link road between two motorways and the more local highways. Gravelly Hill, beyond a spired Methodist church of 1890 in the French Gothic manner of about 1230, has some villas in the late Georgian tradition. Mid-Victorian villas and more modern houses line Kingsbury Road as it approaches one of Birmingham's many agreeable suburban areas. Off Wood End Lane some humble late Georgian cottages stand near Thomason's undistinguished red brick Jaffrey Hospital, opened in 1885.

Erdington was once a hamlet in the great parish of Aston. Barring Church House with its Arts and Crafts Jacobean façade, the High Street contains little of note. The church of 1822-4 and by Rickman and Hutchinson, is unaisled, bulky and clerestoried, with a finely pinnacled west tower and 'Decorated' windows. J. A. Chatwin added the chancel, also the transepts whose arches cant in towards the chancel arch. At the corner of Station Road (which has Georgian cottages and a Methodist chapel by Ewan Harper) the 1858 almshouse buildings of Mason's House are of marked character with a central building and pairs of cottages in simple Tudor Perpendicular.

Along Sutton Road the abbey, with Charles Hansom's adjacent Catholic church (see page 26) is Birmingham's chief conventual building. Now Redemptorist, this monastery block was built to designs by the local architect A. E. Dempster in the years after 1879, by German Benedictines who fled from Bismark's *kulturkampf*. Its style is Decorated, and its sturdy tower has the stamp of authority.

Edwardian housing in Erdington is noticed on page 37. More modern dwellings are on and off Sutton Road. No 111 is a fine pseudo-Elizabethan home in dark red Midland brick. Across the way the modern tower blocks and lower density houses of the Lyndhurst estate rise finely behind a splendid screen of tall trees which the designers, Harry Weedon & Partners, have admirably allowed to survive. Yenton public house is large, of three storeys and simple neo-Jacobean; it is of 1928 by James & Lister Lea. Chester Road, a broad dual carriageway with fine trees in its central spine, runs west between widely varied modern houses and past one good 'Regency' villa towards Pype Hayes.

Region 3
Washwood Heath, Ward End, Saltley and Alum Rock, Shard End, Stechford, Tile Cross.

Past the dingy area of Saltley Viaduct with its derelict gas works, the Derby railway, a canal and the lower Rea, Washwood Heath Road passes a few late Georgian cottages, mid-Victorian workers' housing, and villas with such dates as 1858 and 1860. A Methodist chapel of 1899 has Jacobean terracotta detail and perky little corner turrets in the Harrison Townsend idiom. The Cross Guns Inn is good Jacobean Renaissance. Near Ward End Park with its Victorian Italianate house, a neo-Georgian library finished in 1929 with a complex fanlight was by J. P. Osborne & Son. Ward End church, succeeding a medieval chapel, is small, unimpressive, unaisled 'churchwarden' Early English, with a plain western tower. Normanhurst now a social club is a good late Georgian house, typically Birmingham with hooded window heads and Doric window pillarets.

St Saviour's, Saltley, of 1849-50 and by Hussey who succeeded Rickman, is older than the houses near it. Transeptal and with a good south-western tower, it has widely varied Perpendicular windows. For the nearby college, see pages 27 and 40. Beyond the college the Catholic church (see page 40) was opened in 1934, after bombing it was restored by 1943. Alum Rock Road leading features are the church by Holland Hobbiss (see page 40), the beginnings of the Sutton Dwellings estate, and the Brookhill Inn, well exploiting its triangular site. The road swings north past a fine Georgian house with Gothic touches, and the Pelham Arms Inn, Roman Doric Jacobean dated 1915.

Before Castle Bromwich, amid low-density modern suburbia, the Coleshill road traverses the astonishingly rural expanse of Hodge Hill Common. To the north the church cum social complex consists of two blocks with a lower connecting link. The outside is in pleasing plum-coloured brick. The interior, within the terms of a building meant to intermingle the sacred and the secular, is well thought out; a sloping ramp and the baptistry at its lower end, produce an attractive effect.

Alum Rock Road also leads into Burney Lane where Christ Church, by Holland Hobbiss has a conspicuous capped, rectangular tower. Shard End is a large area of modern housing, mostly low-rise and of low density, with some broad road verges. Near its shopping centre All Saints', by F. J. Osborne and started in 1954, is long, narrow, and basilican. From the east its tower, rectangular and with a tall cupola above its cap, rises above an arch between the church and its attendant hall. The whole grouping, with a canopied figure of Christ and a cross-shaped window, is Germanically picturesque.

Across the river Cole, Stechford has several factories, fine modern swimming baths in Station Road but little else of note. Down Stuart Road a village atmosphere prevails, terracotta tracery graces J. A. Chatwin's All Saints' church, and villas in tree-lined roads give an air of quiet, demure Victorianism.

Beyond Kitt's Green the Tile Cross estate fills one of Birmingham's easterly expanses. The new Catholic church started in 1966 (see page 46 and plate 107) is the most notable building; the cupolas of its Lady Chapel and baptistry effectively foil the upward curves of its concrete roof. Inside it gains much from the design and colours of the symbolic windows by John Chrestien. Behind and above it the Anglican St Peter's is roughly circular, with some top lighting and a gallery, and six bells conspicuous in a rectangular belfry. By Keith Wainwright, it was finished in 1968. Just before the city boundary, garden city ideas conditioned the layout soon after 1956 of the Sheldon Hall estate whose houses are a last version of neo-Georgian. Sheldon Hall Avenue has a wide central strip of grass as it leads towards the hall which is a blend of early Tudor brickwork and building of soon after 1600, with many gables, simply mullioned four-light windows, and larger windows with horizontal transoms.

Region 4
Spring Hill and Hockley, Winson Green, Handsworth

and Handsworth Wood, and Hamstead Hill down to the River Tame.

From the Ladywood Baths of 1940, neo-Georgian with a cupola, a redeveloped area leads to the bottom of Spring Hill where the library (see plate 76) is one of the Martin & Chamberlain office's best works. St Peter's church, clerestoried Perpendicular of 1900 by F. B. Osborn, is less notable than the nearby white-painted, late Georgian terrace. But in Camden Street the school has a particularly striking, alternately glazed and leaded Martin & Chamberlain spire, while nearer Dudley Road, Rickman's lancetted All Saints' church of 1832-3, has no tower but keeps the lower parts of the pinnacles which once gave it a striking silhouette.

The top of Spring Hill crosses Brindley's original, meandering Birmingham Canal and so becomes Dudley Road where the buildings of Dudley Road Hospital, of differing Victorian dates behind Ward's long Gothic frontage of the 1880s, fill an extensive site. A contemporary range lies nearer the road, while extra interest comes from the corner sculpture of Compassion (a woman with her child) by John Bridgeman, set up in 1968. Lee Bridge (see plate 27) crosses Telford's straight canal channel; Barford Road and Dudley Road both have notable Martin & Chamberlain schools among humble Victorian streets and courts, while coloured tiling of the Martin & Chamberlain type appears on three-storeyed houses in Heath Street.

Winson Green Road runs down past the prison to Handsworth New Road with its Arts and Crafts schools by H. T. Buckland who in 1901 succeeded William Martin as the School Board's architect. Its tower is half-timbered like some Worcestershire church towers, and Art Nouveau touches appear in its railings. For the Bishop Latimer church, whose nobly grouped tower and gently canted east end rise proudly above the road, see plate 75. Up Boulton Road the schools, of 1893, are a mediocre Gothic throwback, displaying lower aesthetic standards in the Handsworth School Board than in its Birmingham neighbours. The valley of the Hockley Brook keeps no traces of Soho Pool or of Boulton's historic factory.

A good approach to Handsworth is up Soho Hill or along Hunter's Road. In Hunter's Road Pugin's convent (see page 25) stands opposite the Early English Catholic church by Canon Alexander Scoles, the son of J. J. Scoles, who was both an architect and a priest. Both buildings are less attractive than the late Regency villas with Greek Doric or Ionic doorways, in the same road. Wretham Road, with its suburban villas and neo-Decorated Congregational church, cuts back towards the historic fulcrum of Soho. Villa Road, whose upper end is closed by the ornate façade, and the debased Perpendicular porch of J. G. Dunn's Methodist church of 1900, has some late Regency houses entertainingly grouped slantwise to the road's alignment. Not far across Soho Road Boulton's famous house (see page 13) now serves as a police hostel. Up Soho Road itself the Red Lion Hotel, with a tactically placed cupola at one corner, is typical of Birmingham public-house building of about 1900, ornately Jacobean Renaissance with a Flemish feeling and a bright blend of red and yellow terracotta. Cannon Street Baptist chapel, resited from its more central eighteenth-century position, is dated 1929 and is in the simple, turreted Byzantine style.

Back towards the older part of Handsworth, lower middle class Victorian housing includes ornate Gothic villas of about 1875. North of Handsworth Park, Bromford Close is a bold grouping of contemporary flats in rich red brick.

Hamstead Road starts with the ornate, black and white Art Nouveau fancies of the old Toll Gate House. Victorian and later villadom leads to the old church of Handsworth. A blocked late Norman window and the late Perpendicular northern chapel remain from the medieval building. Most of the rest is J. A. Chatwin's Victorian Gothic. The monuments are good, while three of them make Handsworth church the supreme shrine of the Industrial Revolution. Flaxman's mural to Boulton is artistically the best of the three monuments which commemorate him, Watt and Murdock; Chantrey's Murdock mural, with its bust in a Gothic arch, is less effective than the other two.

Handsworth's northerly reaches have their own interest. Church Lane leads to a district where the Grove Hotel of 1891 is strikingly half-timbered, and where St Andrew's church of 1907-9 shows Bidlake, with few Arts and Crafts touches, pretty strictly in Bodley's Decorated vein; only the pairs of round-headed arches for each bay of his passage aisles show greater originality. The two cottages of the ancient, cruck-supported, and perhaps late medieval 'Town Hall', make a charming survival; beyond it the former Methodist College (see page 28) is Handsworth's most imposing Victorian pile. Down Somerset Road the Methodist chapel, by Crouch and Butler and opened in 1894, has something of the manner of Norman Shaw's London church in Bedford Park; lower down, past late Victorian villas, some charming houses (especially Nos 17 and 19 and one with a corner turret at the end of the road) are minor gems of the Arts and Crafts revival. The pleasant suburb of Handsworth Wood is now well filled by recent groups of flats put up, in deep red or yellow and brown brick, by housing societies. Geoffrey Marks, and John F. Phillips & Partners who designed Bromford Close, are among the architects involved. Some inter-war houses with pleasant brick and tile work in the Hobbiss manner, give a more traditional touch.

Hamstead Hill plunges steeply to the river Tame. Small contemporary houses with singly sloping rooflines, lead to the Elmwood Congregational church, opened in 1969. Its side walls are gently curved, and its western end is almost wholly of glass; the architects were the neighbouring firm of McKavan & McKavan. At the bottom a modern bridge runs parallel to the single, graceful cycloidal arch of Hamstead Bridge of 1809, more sophisticated, but in a worse condition, than Perry Bridge lower down the Tame.

Region 5

Perry Bar, Kingstanding, Old and New Oscott.

Perry Bar starts beyond the ring road where Aston Lane joins Wellington Road. The first landmark is the modern shopping precinct, of good design quality and dominated by the elongated hexagonal tower block of Lynton House, dated 1964 and by J. Brian Cooper and James A. Farquhar; its eastern façade gains interest from a mosaic feature.

The older part of Perry Bar lies between the Walsall and Aldridge roads. The latter has Victorian villas facing some unattractive inter-war semi-detached pairs; between them a central spine retains a row of fine trees. Down by the Tame a good modern dairy depot stands near Perry Bridge with its four round arches, cutwaters, and an approach causeway on one side. It is said to be of 1711 but could be older. Beyond it, past the motorway link road, one approaches a district of low density, neo-Georgian housing; at a crossroads the Boar's Head, built in 1934 to replace an ancient posting inn, is a large, neo-Georgian public house.

Perry Bar's old church, once a chapel in Handsworth parish, was built in 1831-3; its architect (see Aris' *Birmingham Gazette*) was named Studholme. The church has a fine, boldly pinnacled western tower, a simple unaisled nave in a somewhat 'churchwarden' Gothic, and Victorian transepts and chancel. Along Church Road is a nicely taut group of corporation flats, and then the Walsall road and the Tennis Court public house (see plate 91).

Kingstanding is a vast expanse of inter-war corporation housing; some details, such as door canopies, are like those in Weoley Hill where Bournville influences are strong. Pseudo-Georgian, pilastered shopping terraces occur, and a more modern technical college stands across the road from St Matthew's, Perry Beeches (see page 46). The plainly rectangular Catholic church of Christ the King, of 1960-2 and by Jennings, Homer & Lynch, graces one side of what could, with the removal of its central prefabs, be a pleasant oval.

Beyond Kingstanding, in a secluded dip among more modern housing, Old Oscott (later called Maryvale) has a Catholic history going back into penal times. The solid Georgian house, now part of a convent, was built for the priest of the mission; its rectangular chapel, with an Ionic altar-piece, is of 1778. Upstairs, the Sacred Heart chapel of 1814 is Regency Gothic. But the best changes, made when Old Oscott was a college, came a little later. A pilastered assembly hall became the central element of a balanced group including another house, a connecting Roman Doric colonnade, two flanking colonnades, and two charmingly rounded pavilion ends. The old house, the transverse colonnade and the columns on one side of the court survive, but the hall and later side of the court by which John Ireland gave symmetry to the ensemble have been destroyed.

The educational Tudor of the college at New Oscott, recalling the English College at Douai, with its wide *ambulacrum* is noticed on page 24.

Region 6

Deritend, Bordesley, Balsall Heath, Sparkbrook, Sparkhill to the Cole, and Small Heath to the line of Bordesley Green.

This close-built tract of southern Birmingham starts south of the Rea. Except for the Old Crown, Deritend High Street has little character and no merit in its modern buildings. St Anne's Catholic church in Alcester Street is a gaunt Victorian basilica; more interesting is the intended church (see plate 86) built close to the GWR arches by Fr John Lopes as the chapel of a boys' hostel. Dixon, who designed the Byzantine St Basil's not far away, may have been the architect.

Goodwin's Holy Trinity church stands commandingly, at the top of Camp Hill. Houses of late Georgian character survive in Ravenhurst Street, while some Lench Almshouses of 1848, have a pleasantly grouped courtyard in brick and stone, Elizabethan in style. The buildings, once those of the King Edward VI Boys' School, were built in 1883 with two timber spirelets and a richly adorned, geometrical Gothic composition in the Martin & Chamberlain vein. For Stratford House see plate 4. Stratford Place joins Moseley Road near the curved stretch overlooking Highgate Park, where a charming sequence of Regency houses (see p 19) at first gained a charming rural view. More late Georgian houses continue, in an early version of ribbon development, along Moseley Road. Civic buildings here are also of interest. The 'Fire Brigade Station' of 1911 with varied late seventeenth-century references, is by Harrison. For the library-cum-baths complex; see page 34 and plate 85; the library's arcaded hall has a Beaux Arts plaster frieze with classic inspiration. The clock tower looks down on an area, rebuilt with modern blocks of flats and lower houses, where the Baptist chapel-cum-social-centre by Professor Hinton forms a good contemporary religious grouping, and where Pearson's great ambulatory church of St Alban (see plate 60) still rises nobly over the scene. Its style recalls the thirteenth century, and its two main transept windows vary between three lancets in the south and a four-light, plate-traceried northern window. Below it J. A. Chatwin's Lench Almshouses, with their lodge and quadrangle, display Renaissance idioms.

Along Stratford Road, Sparkbrook's architecture has little character, barring a slender-spired school and the splendid tower (see plate 74) and restored body of St Agatha's. To the east, Farm Park, near the mid-Victorian Christ Church with its oddly shaped clerestory windows, is girt by Victorian villas but still contains the modest country house built by the second Sampson Lloyd, the Quaker steel merchant who founded Lloyd's bank. A pedimented front doorway with fluted Doric pilasters, and some characterful window heads, are set in mellow red brick. Baroque fireplaces adorned a mansion put up in 1758, thirteen years after its approach avenue. The more northerly part of Sparkhill has much of interest. The modern Methodist church (see plate 104), the basilican English Martyrs' Catholic church with its campanile, two tasteful Hobbiss public houses, Arthur Harrison's neo-Jacobean Library of 1894, with symbolic figures and a bold, cupola-capped clock tower, and the vaguely modernistic, porticoed baths by Hurley Robinson, started in 1931, make up an entertaining urban collection. More dramatic, inside, is the church of St John the Evangelist by William Martin, dated 1888.

From Sparkbrook, Small Heath lies beyond the BSA factory, across the chasm of the GWR line. It is better approached up Coventry Road past some late Georgian ribbon development, through the St Andrew's area and past Birmingham City's football ground. Drabness is relieved by some Martin & Chamberlain schools, by St Aidan's church, by a little Victorian elaboration on

houses in Herbert Road, and by the library and baths grouping (see plate 77) commenced in 1893. Relief comes round the oasis of Small Heath Park where villas overlook the greenery, and where the tower of Waverley Road's school is among Martin's best. Down in Walford Road, Bidlake's Emmanuel church was started in 1900 and never finished. It has Bodleyan curvilinear windows and a charming Arts and Crafts Gothic turret and spirelet. Back over the park his St Oswald's (see page 36) was started in 1892—his earliest Birmingham church. Down Coventry Road, past slabby ugliness in the erstwhile Singer factory, the Cole, lined with green spaces, is Birmingham's most attractive river.

Region 7

Hall Green, Tyseley, Acock's Green, Yardley, Sheldon.

From the Dingle and its bridge over the Cole, and up tree-lined Highfield Road, one approaches the spacious suburb of Hall Green. After an amusingly 'folksy' house of 1920, a notable building is St Peter's church, by Norman Rider and started in 1962. Its concrete campanile with a cupola has two straight and two concave sides. The church is polygonal, with brick outer walls and a concrete upper stage. Its somewhat darksome interior is notable for its richly tinted glass by Ruhlmann of Strasbourg. The east window shows Christ with sheep and St Peter the fisherman. More unusual are the clerestory windows, with panels in the manner of loosely hung Persian carpets.

The older part of Hall Green has the single-storey Charles Lane almshouses, brick and stone Jacobean of 1936, on the site of the hall once owned by the Marstons. The church, built by them as a 'donative chapel', is Birmingham suburbia's one eighteenth-century church. It is of brick and stone, pilastered and balustraded vernacular baroque of the Warwick school. A three-bay nave and a tower survive from 1703-4. In 1860 the sympathetic transepts and chancel set a precedent for what J. A. Chatwin did at St Philip's. Three galleries stand in a smallish interior, a benefaction board explains the chapel's early history, and contemporary boards set out the allocation of the seating.

The dreary purlieu of Tyseley, intersected by the GWR line and studded with factories, is approached along Warwick Road where Tyseley Methodist church, of 1909 onwards, is Arts and Crafts Perpendicular with a nicely gargoyled tower and spirelet. A more open layout starts before Acock's Green with its bulky, Early English-cum-Geometrical church of 1864 onwards, and still with some village feeling in a diminished 'green' where a pseudo-Elizabethan shopping parade faces the neo-Georgianism and bold chimney stacks of the New Inn and less enterprising neo-Georgianism in the local library. The Catholic church, unaisled and with a pointed barrel roof and an apsidal, timber-vaulted sanctuary, is by G. B. Cox, started in 1939 and belatedly Bidlakean Decorated. Garden city housing and modern flat blocks appear in Dolphin and Woodcock Lanes.

Elsewhere in Acock's Green the Coventry Road crosses the Cole at Hay Mills. A few cottages recall a Georgian past; more exciting are the wire and cable mills built by James Horsfall, and his accompanying architecture of benevolence. A tiny school of 1863 was 'for the edification of the children of his workpeople', while St Cyprian's church, by Chamberlain and of the 1870s, has the Cole flowing beneath it.

South of Acock's Green the Journey's End Inn is good neo-Queen Anne with a hipped roof and four tall chimney stacks. In a vast cemetery the Romanesque chapel, with an octagonal central tower, typifies Birmingham's liking for ambitious funerary churches. South Yardley starts along the Coventry Road. The Tivoli shopping centre, with its three-tier car park and the towering Bakeman House, is by James Roberts and well displays the use of aggregates and cladding panels; it overlooks the well designed underpass, flyover and pedestrian bridge of the outer ring road. South Yardley Methodist church by Botteley and Chaffer, consulting engineers of Sutton Coldfield, is dated 1968. It has a circular porch at the back, good curvature in its main walling, and ingenious hexagonal concrete units in its windows. Further out, the Good Companions public house unhappily mixes mock baroque and the 'modernism' of the 1930s. Residential Rowlands Road is good for the *aficionados* of modern church architecture. Yardley Baptist church, finished in 1966 and by Graham Cochrane, has a rectangular interior with canted ends, downward-sloping seating, and a ceiling which drops towards its dais. At St Michael's church a hall adjoins the vestibule of Professor Hinton's rectangular new building which has boldly curved walls at one end.

At Yardley, Church Road leads past late Georgian cottages and Victorian villas to the old church's delightful setting; here and at King's Norton are Birmingham's best village centres. The church contains all England's medieval Gothic styles. Its best feature is an early Perpendicular tower capped by a slender crocketted spire. The church has some good Georgian murals. Better than these are baroque monuments to the devotedly Royalist parson Humphrey Greswold (d 1671) and the striking composition, with two kneeling figures in a tomblike cavern, to Rev Henry Greswold who died in 1700. The old grammar school, much patched to the south in brick, but with fine late medieval half-timbering and a jettied upper floor, completes the picturesque setting. Blakesley Hall, mid-Tudor, is another manorial survival.

Beyond South Yardley is Sheldon, almost wholly modern in its sprawling growth. Some old cottages and a 'churchwarden' Gothic school are village relics near the old church whose Perpendicular tower once had pinnacles. Its best work, including the font with little cusped arches, is of the fourteenth century. The splendid nave roof, with hammer beams and decorative cinquefoils, is of this time. So too is the great rarity of a pentagonal Decorated window.

The pentagon also appears elsewhere in Sheldon, shaping the main worshipping space in the Catholic church opened in 1970 (see page 47), the district's best modern building. The wooden crucifix and statues, fairly conventional but also devotional, are by Stuflesser of Ortisei in the Tirol. The floor drops slightly towards the sanctuary, and the church gains much from the rich tones and varied designs of the glass by John Chrestien.

Region 8

Moseley, King's Heath, Highter's Heath, Yardley Wood.

From Balsall Heath one reaches Moseley past the inter-war villas of Salisbury Road; a few houses, including No 16 which has an amusing turret and Arts and Crafts Renaissance detail, are earlier. Moseley Hall was built by John Taylor, the partner of Sampson Lloyd II, to replace the mansion which the rioters of 1791 destroyed. Despite hideous mutilation by a northern projection it is one of Birmingham's best late Georgian buildings, delicately detailed with Ionic pilasters, a curved central bow, and pedimented pavilion ends.

Moseley village is nondescript. The best building, with its graceful turret and a barometer and windgauge strangely flanking its doorway, is Newton's Fighting Cocks, designed in 1899. The clerestoried church, with its simple medieval tower outlasting many alterations, is mainly by J. A. and Philip Chatwin, more spacious inside than it looks, blending neo-Decorated and mock Perpendicular. Wake Green Road leads east, past bulky, hideous Victorian villas, and more pleasing Arts and Crafts houses, notably No 31 with its chequered brick and stone and a polygonal turret, and No 50, dated 1907 with a charming cupola above its garage. For the boys' grammar school see pages 27-8 and plate 64. Oxford Road intersects a tract of demure Victorian suburbia; the oval setting of St Agnes', of 1883-4 and 1893 by William Davis, and with a finely pinnacled upper stage of 1932 to its tower, recalls that of St Augustine's, Edgbaston.

Across Alcester Road, and nearer King's Heath, Joseph Chamberlain's Highbury stands neighbour to the neo-Elizabethan Uffculme, dated 1890 and with an Ionic portico. The 'village' of King's Heath is generally undistinguished. A Baptist chapel has a large wheel window above twin arches in the manner of about 1200, while at the corner of York and Heathfield Roads two banks have turrets capped by spirelets, which exploit corner sites in a typically local way; one has a doorway in elaborate French late Gothic. The spired parish church is run of the mill mid-Victorian Gothic; for the recent Catholic church see page 46 and plate 106. Down Vicarage Road the Red Lion, originally built by the Cartlands and dated 1903-4, has a stone front richly blending late Gothic and Renaissance ornament.

To the east a garden city feeling, with widely varied inter-war villas, trees and wide grass verges, prevails towards Swanshurst Park. Down by the Cole, Sarehole Mill is a delightful, lately restored rural and industrial survival. Matthew Boulton used it for metal working in his pre-Soho days. It has buildings in Georgian red brick, doveholes in one gable, a square chimney, and small-paned metal windows.

Beyond King's Heath, Victorian villas and some with an Arts and Crafts flavour line the main road through a low-density suburban townscape. Cocks Moor Woods make a fine sylvan belt, and the Maypole district comes just before the Worcestershire border. Its Methodist church, started in 1960, has patterned brickwork and a slender corner tower. Near it is the beginning of a great cluster of terrazzo-clad blocks of flats, mixed with a few shops, a social centre in dark red brick, and some lower-rise housing, which stretches towards King's Norton. The Maypole Inn of 1935, marks the end of Birmingham with its early Tudor style and fine brick chimney stacks. At Highter's Heath a little salient contains Immanuel church. By Harvey & Wicks, it was started in 1939 and conceals a plain, simply piered interior, and a beautiful baroque vase font of marble, behind a broad Romanesque façade.

At Yardley Wood the Stratford Canal runs in a deep cutting and is spanned by an imposing, high-arched, red brick bridge. The church has a charming western tower, a low spire, and simple lancet detail; it is by A. E. Perkins, prolific on Victorian work in Worcester diocese which then contained it. Close by, a pair of Gothic cottages of 1857 house John Cotterill's Charity (of 1715) for two poor widows. The village school has Dutch Renaissance details and a Wrennish cupola. Lower down, the Haven Inn of 1929 strikingly combines half-timbering with red and blue brick. Stone plaques of a windmill and a ship adorn its late Tudor idiom. It is by Holland Hobbiss; its notably patterned, East Anglian chimney stacks resemble those on the same architect's contemporary University Students' Union. The nearby library is neo-Georgian, dated 1936, and with clerestory lighting for its radiating interior. Above its doorway one finds a globe, stylised clouds, cherubs' busts and an open book inscribed SAPERE AUDE. At the top of the pretty wooded Dingle, a three-arched bridge of brick spans the Cole.

Region 9

Edgbaston and part of Ladywood.

Edgbaston starts at the fork of Calthorpe and Harborne Roads where a fine late Georgian house in the typical Birmingham manner has, at its back, a sensitively designed block in good modern brick. By the Madin Group, it has a rear elevation gently curved along a short loop road.

This initial district is a surprisingly successful blend of late Georgian houses and more massive modernity. Calthorpe Road starts with charming late Georgian houses of brick or stucco-fronted. But Shell-BP House, of 1961-2 and like other nearby office blocks by the Madin Design Group which supervises the Calthorpe estate's development, is modern, L-shaped with the blank end of its taller block facing the road, and striking in its black and cream effect. Harborne Road also starts with Regency or Victorian villas, but where it meets Highfield Road the new Chamber of Commerce building is impressively sited, L-shaped, and with cleanly designed, tasteful interiors to complement its external quality. Frederick Road, and others near it, retain their Regency or early Victorian aspect.

In Hagley Road the tower block of Calthorpe House rises above the Edgbaston shopping precinct with its good piazza. The similarly planned tower blocks of Hagley and Lyndon Houses, bright with their cladding of white marble mosaic, stand assertively on each side of the highway. Late Georgian houses, individually or in short terraces, recall earlier development; one has lower windows divided by typically local Roman Doric pillarets. Some lower modern office blocks contrast with the more massive towers. They too are by Madin; in one of them (plate 95), the massing of whose brickwork resembles their graduate hall of residence for the university, this architectural group has its offices. The AA building (plate 101) next to a fine villa graced by a Greek Doric porch, is another striking modern work. The rambling, mullioned neo-Tudor Plough and Harrow Hotel echoes Edgbaston's more romantic past. Plough and Harrow Road, with its vista to Perrott's Folly, leads towards Ladywood; on the corner site a modern office block, close against the Oratory House, unhappily darkens Newman's carefully preserved room which is Birmingham's most eloquent personal shrine.

Along Monument Road, Ladywood has a 'village' feeling; some pleasant stuccoed villas of about 1850 survive in Reservoir Road, while in Harold Road, Tillstock Villas of 1892, display terracotta in the mullions, capitals, and rosettes of Gothic first-floor windows.

The Oratory, the Church of the Redeemer, and more modern office and flat blocks are prominent in Hagley Road. North of it one is no longer in Calthorpe territory. Densities are higher, but an essentially suburban character remains in Rotton Park. In Rotton Park Road and in the nearer parts of Hagley Road, villas and rows of houses in mid-Victorian red brick, convey a north Oxford flavour. The reservoir is the city's largest sheet of water. At one corner a single-arched Georgian bridge is a miniature of those which cross the canals.

Residential growth continues on each side of Hagley Road. No 431 which has a rainwaterhead of 1907, is good Arts and Crafts with its two-storeyed bow, an oriel, and a pattern of chequered brick and stone. Hermitage Road has a piquant contrast between the distinguished flats block of West Point and some romantic Tudor cottages.

In central Edgbaston, Vicarage and Carpenter Roads are good for stuccoed late 'Regency' villas, Greek Doric and Ionic both featuring in their doorways and porches. Edgbaston Hall, near the squat medieval tower of the old church, is somewhat disappointing as an early Georgian country house. Brick-built, it has a fine grand staircase; good external features are heraldic rainwaterheads with the Gough arms.

Central Edgbaston was laid out by the amenity-conscious Calthorpes, as an uncommercial, low-density suburb of large villas, Italianate or Gothic, in the privacy of spacious gardens. The Jacobean-Renaissance pile of the Blind Institute (now Broadcasting House) was among the few public buildings, but many large houses have lately disappeared. Precincts and closes of smaller, more closely built modern houses, as one sees off Augustus Road, now occupy their garden sites. Infilling has also occurred in areas once unoccupied, but careful supervision has ensured that this greater density does not offend the character of so beautiful a suburb. A triangular shopping precinct by Harry Bloomer & Son, is another new feature.

Below Church Road a sloping, beautifully landscaped precinct contains five university halls of residence and is much improved by a new lake. High Hall, by Harvey & Wicks and finished in 1964, is a tall block, with a common room and a dining hall in its podium, attractively capped and with pleasingly treated corners varying its brick expanses. The adjacent Ridge Hall is lower; Lake and Wyddrington Halls are tautly enclosed precincts. Mason Hall, with one tower block and the newest of the group, stands near the lower end of the lake. In Edgbaston Park Road the Extra-mural Department is in a house dated 1903 by C. L. Ball; it has a coved cornice, finely patterned Wrenaissance brickwork, and arched chimney stacks.

The University's early buildings, and some built since 1945, feature on pages 37-8 and 47-8. The congested effect of the older part is much less pronounced north of Pritchatt's Road; buildings there are better seen, and more happily display their architectural qualities than do those nearer the original blocks. Up the road the sequence starts with the attractive three-sided court of the Health Centre. Near it the departments of Metallurgy and Minerals Engineering share three-tiered buildings by Arup Associates. Their silhouette suffers from the unattractive caps which top the concrete uprights, but the buildings, in concrete, red brick and dark glass, have a fine structural integrity, reminding me of their architects' residential hostels for two Cambridge colleges. Professor Hinton's linked blocks for Electronic and Electrical Engineering are an interesting pair, one with a facing mainly of black bricks, the other with shallow bricks in a pleasing grey; their skyline is marked by a bizarre but needful radio telescope. Lower down, one end of Casson & Conder's Department of Education has varied, very fine grouping of the irregularly placed brick masses which face the road. An enclosed rose garden is among the building's agreeable features as one passes it towards the Barber Institute and the fine equestrian statue of George I which, in 1722, graced Essex Bridge in Dublin.

Region 10
Selly Oak, Bournville and Weoley Hill, Weoley Castle, Bartley Green.

Along Bristol Road, Selly Oak starts soon after the University. A good Gothic pumping station by Chamberlain, and J. P. Osborn's Arts and Crafts Renaissance library of 1905, introduce the shopping suburb, the wierdly oriental silhouette of some hospital blocks, and Holmes' Victorian Gothic church. To the south is the residential suburbia of Selly Park. Here too, in a park-like setting, is another typical, spired mid-Victorian suburban church, this time by Martin & Chamberlain and of 1870-1. The Victorian buildings of a large convent complex include a Puginesque Gothic gateway and a convent block, in deep red brick with crosses picked out in blue. Some Arts and Crafts houses appear in Selly Park Road, notably Nos 55 and 57 with deep, almost colonial American, Roman Doric porches.

The Selly Oak colleges include a Georgian mansion, Harvey's Fircroft built for the younger George Cadbury, and purpose-built educational blocks mostly by Harvey & Wicks. The most convincingly collegiate, with a chapel, is the College of the Ascension, of the 1920s, for training Anglican deaconesses. All are within the Bournville zone. One soon reaches the spacious, well planted, pioneering garden city; contemporary infilling and extension now complete the residential pattern. The estate's older, more social parts and the factory build-

ings are well known. The almshouses, of 1897 by Ewan Harper, are older than Harvey's village buildings. Pseudo-Elizabethan and spaciously grouped on a traditional, quadrangular plan, they are less 'arty' and self-conscious than the buildings round the leafy green. There the Quakers' Meeting House, the later, Romanesque basilican church, the shopping parade, Ruskin Hall, the continuation schools, and the main schools with their sturdy tower and varied Gothic or Renaissance details, combine with trees and street furniture to form a most attractive Arts and Crafts period piece. Among the few blemishes are the copper cupola above its school tower, added in 1934 to hold a carillon, and the 'Rest House', modelled on Dunster's Yarn Market but neither effective nor a good imitation.

The Bournville estate, bought piecemeal, was never planned as a whole, but residential areas are related, with parkways between them. Some of the Bournville Village Trust's ventures lie north of Bristol Road, and Weoley Hill, started before 1914, has some brick houses finished in pebble dash. This area's best feature, leading to the step-gabled Presbyterian church of the 1930s, is the noble avenue, graced by a central spine of trees, of Middle Park Road. Princethorpe Avenue is a tree-lined dual carriageway. At its foot, near a wooded circle and a pool, the Catholic church of 1959 by Adrian Gilbert Scott has an imposing eliptical arch outside its western tower.

Weoley Castle was the most important medieval secular building in what is now Birmingham. In 1264 the de Somerys enclosed the fortified space with a stone wall containing a gatehouse and five rectangular projecting towers. Excavation has shown that well into that century there was still the comparative rarity of an important, hall-like timber building, with weather boarding between its wooden uprights.

Region 11
Harborne and Quinton.

Harborne was long a Staffordshire country parish; what caused its suburbanisation was the opening in 1874 of the branch line of the L & NWR. A village atmosphere still pervades its centre; a few late Georgian cottages survive, particularly in Vivian Road, amid Victorian buildings and a pretentious, pseudo-baroque public house of 1903. More interesting, north of the main village and not far from a district of inter-war houses in a restless variety of designs, is the Harborne Tenants' estate (see page 37), covering 54 acres; its houses number about 500.

Round the old churchyard there is still a good village precinct. The church, with a simple late medieval tower, some late Georgian murals, and good benefaction boards, was mostly rebuilt in the French Gothic of about 1200, by Yeoville Thomason; it is mediocre even by his standards. Bishop's Croft, not far away, is a fine Georgian mansion, better than Edgbaston Hall, of mellow red brick, with Adamesque detail on two doorways, and embellished in the 1920s by a chapel to Dixon's designs. In Vivian Road the Catholic church, mostly Early English and with fine trefoil-headed eastern lancets, is Birmingham's surviving church by Edward Hansom and A. M. Dunn.

The convent and retreat house of Harborne Hall are a restless, irregular and messy mid-Victorian complex in unattractive red brick. Off the splendidly leafy dual avenue of Harborne Park Road the modern offices, in attractive brickwork, of Birmingham's Anglican diocese are a nice achievement by Bromilow, While & Smeeton. Cross Farm Road, cutting back towards Edgbaston, has attractive low density housing, individually or in terraces, and at the top some tower blocks of flats. In Metchley Lane the best feature is the 'Romantic' or 'churchwarden' Gothic Metchley 'Abbey', where a panelled parapet blends with windows whose tracery is no more than an intersection of glazing bars.

Beyond Lordswood Road which leads spaciously down to Harborne, Hagley Road is the border between suburban Birmingham and Warley. The Hollybush Inn, opposite yet another neo-Georgian shopping parade, has strong baroque touches to adorn its revivalist Queen Anne style. In Quinton village the church of 1840, aisleless and in a simple lancet style, has a turret capped by a spirelet. The village itself displays nothing of note; to the south, towards the upland area of World's End, low-density post-war houses surround St Boniface's church, rectangular, with a high-pitched roof and brickwork in attractive patterns and colours. Its western turret, with copper mellowed to green, is a characterful work by Bromilow, While & Smeeton.

Region 12

King's Norton, Northfield, Longbridge.

The approach to King's Norton first reaches Cotteridge, where the tower of St Agnes' church dominates Pershore Road. The main building, started in 1902 and by Cossins, Peacock & Bewlay, is ordinary enough, with an apsed sanctuary and stone nave pillars below brick arches. More interesting is the finely composed tower with Arts and Crafts Gothic detail, which recalls Bidlake's tower at his Bishop Latimer church. Cotteridge also has its recent Quakers' Meeting House cum social centre, and a psuedo-Queen Anne fire station dated 1930, with urns and a swan's neck pediment.

King's Norton has an attractive village green a genuine growth, less contrived than that of Bournville. One side has the long, low, plastered and half-timbered range of the old Saracen's Head; beyond the church the old grammar school is of brick and stone in its lower storey, and has a debased Gothic stone doorway and a timber-framed upper storey with medieval woodwork from the building's parsonage days. In the spacious church the long, low nave has seven bays of about 1300 with two differing arcades; on its sunny side it has an array of Stuart gables and mullioned windows. The monuments, though good, are less outstanding than at Aston or Yardley, and the church's conspicuous glory is its Perpendicular western tower, adorned with niches on its village side, richly parapetted and capped by a crocketted spire which is a richer version of that at Yardley. In the village the terracotta baroque School Board offices of 1901, and the multigabled school recall King's Norton's Worcestershire days. Near the railway the Triplex office tower (see page 44) is the area's best modern building, while down towards the housing zone of West Heath is a small modern shopping parade.

Across the Rea the old village of Northfield has much character and group value. Georgian cottages surround the church, and the 'churchwarden' Gothic school is dated 1837. Late Norman relics apart, the church's nave has two arcades, one genuine Decorated, the other, by Bodley, more elaborately in the same style. The thirteenth-century chancel (see plate 2) is Birmingham's most refined medieval building. Up on the Bristol road, amid varied housing, one finds modern shops, neo-Georgian baths of 1937 with a square cupoletto, a finely towered modern Methodist church by J. P. Osborne, and C. E. Bateman's ornate, mainly black and white Black Horse Inn in the domestic style of 1500. Further out, the great brick and terracotta Martin & Martin tower of the Hollymoor Asylum attracts attention by its lofty copper dome.

At Longbridge the modern church of St John the Baptist, by G. H. While, lies east of the main road. Akin to that at Quinton, it has a copper-capped tower. Bristol Road bears off towards Rubery, and the pumping house tower (see plate 78) keeps company with British Leyland's most recent canteen. The Methodist church by Clifford Downing, was finished in 1967 and is of marked quality though somewhat dark inside. A charming courtyard leads to its irregularly octagonal worshipping space, top-lit from an upward-rising roof and well furnished on a modern plan. A co-operative shop of the 1930s has nicely varied brickwork and a rounded corner tower. The Longbridge Inn is simple inter-war Jacobean, and the well landscaped Rubery Hill Hospital has none of its Victorian brick buildings equivalent to Hollymoor's tower

The Longbridge motor works, stretching over the Worcestershire border, are among the city's most important groupings. Pages 44-5 deal with many post-war changes in the great complex of factories, offices, showrooms and social buildings. Yet none of this work is more impressive than the little shrine in the new engineering block, near the buildings which Herbert Austin bought in 1905. For there, lovingly reinstated is Austin's office, cosily panelled, furnished in a homely way, with books and other objects from long before their owner became a great captain of industry. The room is an industrial parallel to Thomas Hardy's study, reassembled from Max Gate, in the museum at Dorchester.

Biographical Notes

The short biographies which follow do not include architects who have mainly worked in Birmingham since 1914, or who are still alive. Architects like Archer, Pearson, Beazley, Barry, or Aston Webb and Ingress Bell who designed a few important Birmingham buildings though mainly based on London are therefore excluded. So too are more local men, like the Hiorns, Eykyn, and Horton who were only certainly responsible for a single Birmingham building. One must, however, remember that Birmingham architects, based in the chief city of the Midlands and the second largest in England, have designed many buildings outside their own city. This applies, in particular, to Victorian architects, and to most of those now in practice in Birmingham.

Pre-Victorian

WILLIAM HOLLINS came of a Midland family, perhaps from near Worcester, but moved to Birmingham as a child and lived there for over seventy years till his death in 1843. He was self-educated, and made a careful study of Vitruvius as well as being interested in lettering. His work in Birmingham included the Old Library in Union Street, the initial building, in 1806, of the Public Office, the Union Street Dispensary of 1806-8, the Athenaeum in Temple Street which later became for some years the headquarters of the Birmingham Society of Artists, and some enlargements of the church at Handsworth. He refused an offer to enter the service of the Tsar of Russia, but made some designs for a mint in St Petersburg.

Hollins was a sculptor as well as an architect, and the older churches of Birmingham contain several of his mural monuments. His son Peter became a sculptor of national standing, and some of his statues, busts and mural monuments exist in Birmingham.

JOHN RAWSTHORNE. A pupil of James Wyatt who established himself in Birmingham late in the eighteenth century. His scheme for the Crescent, in association with Charles Norton who later designed Christ Church, came out in 1790. He designed the Cavalry Barracks in 1792, and in 1792-4 he was the architect for the new buildings of the Blue Coat School. Rawsthorne later practised in Doncaster and designed the Royal Infirmary at Sheffield.

THOMAS RICKMAN (1776–1841). Rickman was one of the most important architects ever to work in Birmingham. A Quaker, born in Berkshire, he had a varied career as a chemist, a doctor's assistant, a doctor, and in a London corn merchant's office before he moved to Liverpool and there worked as a clerk in the office of an insurance broker. His initial interest in architecture was that of an enthusiastic and studious amateur, as a self-taught draughtsman, and as a widely travelled visitor to churches and other buildings. While still in the Liverpool insurance business he lectured on architecture to the Liverpool Academy, and his article (of 1812-15) for Smith's *Panorama of Arts and Sciences* was reprinted in 1817 as 'An Attempt to Discriminate the Styles of English Architecture'. Rickman here coined the terms Norman, Early English, Decorated and Perpendicular for the main medieval styles seen in England.

In 1812 Rickman met Thomas Cragg, a Liverpool ironfounder who was an obvious enthusiast for the architectural use of cast iron. Together they evolved designs for the cast-iron pillars, roof structure and window tracery of St George's church at Everton which was started in 1814. Similar details, along with some exterior ironwork, appeared in the contemporary Liverpool church of St Michael's in the Hamlet. In 1817 Rickman set up as an architect in Liverpool. Henry Hutchinson, his first pupil (whose elder brother had already worked as an architect in Birmingham) became his partner in 1821, and remained for ten years until his early death. In St George's church Rickman had already had his first Birmingham commission. He opened a Birmingham office in 1820, and from 1821 lived in Birmingham. His brother Edwin was for a time his assistant, but was later replaced by R. C. Hussey who became Rickman's partner and his eventual successor.

Rickman and his partners had a large and busy practice, with churches and other buildings in Worcestershire and Warwickshire, at St John's College, Cambridge, and at Loughborough, Bristol and Clevedon, as well as their buildings in Birmingham mentioned on pages 20 and 21. Though Rickman's name is chiefly associated with the various medieval styles, he was also highly competent as a classical designer. Churches, not all Gothic were a large item in Rickman's output, and some of his fellow Quakers criticised his attendance at their consecration ceremonies as an 'encouragement of superstitious rites'. Apart from such jobs as the survey of King Edward VI School, Rickman's office drew up plans for various unexecuted buildings, for example, for an Ionic town hall, and a large Catholic church to replace the original St Chad's; and also designs for markets, a news room, and a post office. Thomas Rickman, having handed his work over to R. C. Hussey, died in 1841.

SAMUEL WYATT (1737–1807). A member of the large family of late Georgian and Victorian builders and designers, the third son of Benjamin Wyatt of Weeford near Lichfield and thus an elder brother of the better known James Wyatt. He early followed his father's trade, and had country house commissions from 1776 onwards, about the time when he set up his important and prosperous designing and building practice in London. Trinity House was among his important London buildings; he also designed the Commissioner's House in Portsmouth Dockyard as well as being the Clerk of Works at the Royal Hospital in Chelsea. His importance for Birmingham's architecture came from his frequent employment by the firm of Boulton & Watt. He could, in his early days, have worked on the original buildings at Soho, and he must have been well known to Boulton when in 1777 the master of Soho recommended him as 'a proper person' to design the new façade for the Theatre Royal. The Albion Mills near Blackfriars Bridge in London, pioneeringly powered by Boulton & Watt engines which were later destroyed by incendiaries, were among his most important Boulton & Watt commissions. He also reconstructed and refaced Soho House in the simple neo-classical style which he normally favoured, and designed Heathfield as a residence for Watt. In 1801 he took out a patent for the construction of bridges and other structures of iron.

Victorian and Later

JOHN JONES and C. E. BATEMAN. The son of Joseph B. Bateman, himself a Birmingham architect, who may be one of the two 'surveyors' T. and J. Bateman, mentioned in a Birmingham directory of 1818; another directory, of 1837, lists a surveyor named Joseph Bateman who was presumably this architect's father. J. J. Bateman himself worked on a wide range of buildings, mostly in various Gothic styles. His best known church is the Unitarian Church of the Messiah in Broad Street, built in 1861-2. The apsidal St Cuthbert's, Winson Green was ten years later. He was the architect of a bank, a workhouse just off Dudley Road, a hotel, and some branch libraries. He specialised in domestic work, with houses at King's Heath and elsewhere which were 'purposely of a comfortable yet inexpensive character'. Bateman was the first President of the Birmingham Architectural Association and died, aged 85, in 1903. His son C. E. Bateman was then his partner, and one imagines that the younger man was responsible, about 1902, for the unexecuted designs for two commercial buildings, one in Cannon Street and the other in Cornwall Street, which were to have had steel and concrete frames behind towering Flemish-Renaissance façades. C. E. Bateman also designed a house for his father at Castle Bromwich. The partners competed for the new church of St Agatha, and in 1914 C. E. Bateman assessed the competition for St Germain's in Edgbaston. He practiced till well after the end of the World War I, making a name for large public houses, for attractive houses in the Arts and Crafts manner, and for church screens at Erdington, Walsall, Towyn and elsewhere.

WILLIAM HENRY BIDLAKE who died aged 76 in 1938, had by then retired to Sussex from his busy career in Birmingham. His father was a builder-designer at Wolverhampton, and some of his early training was in his father's office. He was at Christ's College, Cambridge, continued training under his father, but later, significantly, trained under Bodley. He became keen on English Gothic, particularly that of the fourteenth century, and Bodley's influence is very clear in much of his church work. He widened his experience after gaining the Pugin Travelling Studentship of the RIBA.

Bidlake settled in Birmingham in 1887 and actively encouraged students and art workers. He was a leading figure in the Birmingham Guild of Handicrafts whose headquarters, at Kyrle Hall, he designed. Apart from this he was the real originator in Birmingham of systematic architectural education. Till about 1893 the local training of architects had been much neglected, and it was about that time that Bidlake was appointed as a lecturer in architectural history in the Day School of Architecture which formed part of the Birmingham Municipal School of Art. He later became the school's director, remaining in the post till 1924; many architects who practised in Birmingham owed some of their training to him.

Though he disliked Art Nouveau, declaring that 'we do not want a new style', Bidlake admired Norman Shaw and became a keen member of the Arts and Crafts movement, regretting the decay of traditional arts and crafts and encouraging their revival by members of his Handicrafts Guild. *The Modern Home*, by Bidlake, Halsey Ricardo and John Cash, published in 1906 as part of the Art and Life Library, shows how much Bidlake stood at the centre of this phase of English taste. Bidlake's own chapter, on 'The House From Outside', outlines his own idealistic beliefs, and among those who contributed illustrations of their buildings and furniture were such key figures as Ernest Newton, Lutyens, Voysey, Walter Crane, Guy Dawber, Frank Brangwyn, William Morris, Baillie Scott, Aston Webb, Barnsley, Ashbee, Gimson, Detmar Blow and his partner Ferdinand Billerey, E. S. Prior, and Morley Horder; C. E. Bateman was a Birmingham contributor.

Bidlake was important as the designer of charming individual houses in and around Birmingham and in the Bristol area and elsewhere, in the Arts and Crafts tradition. Like C. E. Bateman and his pupil W. A. Harvey, he is one of the Birmingham architects whose work is illustrated in Hermann Muthesius' *Das Englische Haus* of 1905-6. Most of his sensitive, original church work is an Arts and Crafts version of Bodley's late Gothic, though he used Romanesque, with a striking entrance composition, in his Congregational church at Sparkhill. C. E. Bateman, in two obituary notices, describes Bidlake as an ambidextrous draughtsmen with a fine eye for colour. His deafness and poor health made him more and more elusive and retiring in his later years.

JOHN H. CHAMBERLAIN was born in Leicester in 1831, the son of a Calvinistic Baptist minister. He early showed an interest in the arts, and became an enthusiastic disciple of Ruskin. He was articled to Goddard of Leicester and finished his training in London; he was, by now, an enthusiast for Italian Gothic. In 1856 he settled in Birmingham where his uncle had been the head of a firm for which he soon designed a strikingly Gothic shop in Union Street. His first few years of architectural practice were difficult and chequered. He was largely supported by commissions from places other than Birmingham, as Birmingham, to quote his obituary in *The Architect*, 'did not take kindly to architectural art'. After some work for Lord Lyttelton, and at Uppingham, Leicester and elsewhere, he nearly emigrated to New Zealand, but in 1864 he entered into a fruitful partnership with William Martin. He became Professor of Architecture at Queen's College and was, from 1865, the honorary secretary of the Birmingham and Midland Institute.

Various public buildings were among the most important Martin & Chamberlain commissions. The offices and board schools for the Birmingham School Board were noteworthy; in addition there were police stations, baths and some of the pumping stations put up for the Birmingham Waterworks. The School of Art in Margaret Street was one of Chamberlain's last commissions, and at the time of his death he was looking forward to the laying of its foundation stone. From 1878 onwards Martin & Chamberlain were also the surveyors for Joseph Chamberlain's urbanistic venture of Corporation Street. Though J. H. Chamberlain was not a relative of Joseph Chamberlain he was much in contact with the leading public figure in Victorian Birmingham. He was a natural choice as the architect of Joseph Chamberlain's mansion of Highbury, and for William Kenrick's house, The Grove at Harborne whose decoratively panelled polygonal anteroom is now in the Victoria and Albert Museum. Chamberlain also designed two Birmingham churches, and a Methodist chapel was one of his earliest buildings.

Chamberlain was prominent in Birmingham's civic and cultural life. He was a good public speaker and lecturer, and his friendship with William Morris enabled him to get Morris as a lecturer at the Birmingham and Midland Institute. Not long before his death he became a magistrate. He died very suddenly in 1883, aged only 52 and at the peak of his career.

JULIUS ALFRED CHATWIN, the son of a Birmingham button manufacturer, was born in the city in 1830. Part of his schooling was at King Edward VI School where he learnt to draw, and where the drawing master did designs for buildings. After a time at an Academy of Arts in Temple Row he started work with the local building contractors Branson & Gwyther; while he was with them he decided to become an architect. The firm put him in touch with various clients, and his first houses, an Italianate pair of villas, dated from 1850. Another of his early buildings is the severely classical Bingley Hall, built for shows, exhibitions and similar functions and involving the use of materials earlier meant for stations and other railway works.

In 1851 Chatwin was articled to Charles Barry. He was in Barry's office for four years, started practice in Birmingham in 1855, visited Italy in 1857, and continued to work on houses. His subsequent practice was that of a prolific designer both of churches (almost wholly Gothic) and of secular buildings of which the majority displayed a variety of Renaissance idioms. He was the leading designer of new Anglican churches in Victorian Birmingham, but his best work was the new chancel of St Philip's, sympathetic to Archer's work and respectful of his training under the essentially Italianate Barry. Apart from his new buildings Chatwin was also active on the restoration of churches, at St Mary's, Warwick, at Kidderminster and elsewhere. He designed new buildings for commercial firms and banks, and worked much for Lloyd's Bank both on new buildings and on the adaptation of existing premises; on these commissions he normally employed a somewhat ornate Renaissance style. As an old boy and as a pupil of Barry he was, in 1866, appointed architect to King Edward VI School; among his unexecuted commissions one of considerable interest and excitement was a glass palace for an Indian maharajah.

J. A. Chatwin had a good collection of pictures and was Chamberlain's successor as a vice-president of the Birmingham Society of Artists. He died in 1907; the practice (still active in Birmingham in the family name) was carried on by his son Philip Chatwin who died, aged ninety-one, in 1964. Like his father, Philip Chatwin did distinguished work on church restoration, and fulfilled several commissions for Lloyd's Bank. He was also the architect, not long before World War I, of the massively Renaissance King Edward VI Girls' Grammar School at Handsworth.

JETHRO ANSTICE COSSINS was a Somerset man, educated at Taunton and Castle Cary; a visit to Wells Cathedral inspired him to become an architect. He was articled to a London architect who later moved to Birmingham. He worked in various Birmingham offices, eventually coming to the notice of Sir Josiah Mason who commissioned him to design Mason College; for this purpose he visited many continental schools and colleges. He also designed the old Liberal Club in Edmund Street, repaired Aston Hall, and did various ecclesiastical work. He took F. B. Peacock as a partner in 1887, in 1900 his nephew Herbert Bewlay, and on Herbert Bewlay's death his brother Ernest Bewlay. He was an enthusiast for church antiquities, intensively studied old Warwickshire churches, and was a local agent for the Society for the Protection of Ancient Buildings. He was 'too much of an archaeologist to crave for dubious originality.' He died, aged eighty-eight, in 1917.

ARTHUR STANSFIELD DIXON (1856-1929) was the eldest son of George Dixon, a prominent man in Birmingham's civic and political circles, a keen educationist, and a close associate of Joseph Chamberlain. George Dixon was mayor, an MP for Birmingham, and for twenty years the chairman of the Birmingham School Board which commissioned the Martin & Chamberlain schools. Dixon went, before his architectural training, to Rugby and University College, Oxford, was also a friend of William Morris and Philip Webb, and was an accomplished silversmith and copper worker. He was prominent in the Birmingham Guild of Handicrafts Ltd which worked on parallel lines to the guild established by Bidlake. He designed its building in Great Charles Street, with a charmingly simple brick frontage of about 1895.

Dixon's practice included general work, but he specialised in churches both in Birmingham and the surrounding districts; he also designed an Anglican cathedral at Seoul in Korea. His best known church in Birmingham is St Basil's in Deritend.

CHARLES EDGE, who died in 1867, was trained and started his career in the late Georgian Grecian tradition but ended as a Victorian architect working both in Italianate and Gothic, his Gothic designs being mainly for churches. His best known Birmingham works were the Market House and his completion of the Town Hall. Apart from his private practice he had several municipal commissions, and got out designs for a Birmingham business man who had development interests at Filey on the Yorkshire coast. He is the only Birmingham architect of his period to have left a large collection of surviving drawings. The four volumes of designs by Charles Edge, and by his son Charles Allerton Edge who was more committedly (and unhappily) a Victorian Gothicist, are in the City Reference Library. They suggest that Charles Edge was mainly responsible for the attractive late Grecian development of Bennett's Hill, and reveal his stylistic development from strict Grecian revivalism to Italianate work. They show that Joseph Hansom was for a time Edge's associate, and that Yeoville Thomason was in his office.

OLIVER ESSEX (1855–1939) was a Birmingham man who trained under W. H. Ward and always practised in Birmingham, with a London office as well as his Birmingham headquarters. He was the head of the partnership of Essex, Nichol & Goodman whose best work, for a few years before and after 1900, was in a mixture of brick and terracotta, with a stylistic emphasis on Flemish Renaissance. The meat market, and the slaughter house with its conspicuous brick and terracotta tower and a starting date of 1895, are among the firm's most important surviving buildings. Another, only recently demolished and with a striking cupola and two great gables in its Suffolk Street frontage, and an elaborate main doorway, was the Technical School whose design was published in 1893.

WILLIAM ALEXANDER HARVEY was a pupil of Bidlake at the Municipal School of Art; he had also studied architecture in Italy, Spain, Germany and the USA. While still a young man he was employed by George Cadbury to design houses in the Bournville Village. For a few years from 1900, at a vital time for the building up of the model village, he was the employee of the Bournville Village Trust and remained its consultant architect after he had started in private practice. For his work at Bournville and elsewhere he was widely hailed as a pioneering designer in the Arts and Crafts tradition, and he was much respected by Muthesius (who illustrated one of his houses in *Das Englische Haus*) and other continental critics. From 1914 he worked, with Graham Wicks, on a wide range of work including churches, housing schemes, schools, banks, a town hall at Dudley, and barracks for the War Office. He died, aged 76, in 1951.

WILLIAM HENMAN was the son of an architect and had an architect brother who collaborated with him in some of his hospital work. He did various work in Birmingham and its neighbourhood, including some late Victorian houses, the Midland Hotel, some business chambers in the area of Cornwall Street, a Renaissance insurance office in Colmore Row, and part of a library, in 1906, for the Aston Local Board: the last named building is restrained Jacobean, with a striking tower on one corner, and pleasant railings in the Arts and Crafts tradition. Henman's best known building, still imposing despite many changes, is the General Hospital, for which he won a competition in 1892. *The Builder*, in its comment on the neo-Jacobean design with its towers, arcades and other embellishments (all rendered in a fiercely red terracotta not unlike that of the Law Courts) made the point that 'Architectural effect has been combined with practical arrangement and construction more completely and successfully than is usual in large hospital buildings'. Henman specialised in hospital work, and wrote and lectured on this aspect of architecture. He died in 1917.

WILLIAM MARTIN was born in Somerset in 1829, was articled to a Birmingham architect named Plevins, and became a partner of D. R. Hall who designed Winson Green Prison. J. H. Chamberlain joined this practice in 1864, and apart from their work for the School Board the firm carried out much municipal work for the rest of the century. Martin, who eventually took his son Frederick into partnership, continued the practice after Chamberlain's premature death in 1883, and it is important to remember that many of the Chamberlain & Martin schools, including that in Waverley Road, Small Heath, of 1892 with a noble square tower which has corner pinnacles and a pierced spirelet, date from the period when Martin was working on his own; the same applies to the church of St John the Evangelist, Sparkhill, unusual for the striking effect of its central space.

Martin, who died in 1900, was the assessor in various architectural competitions His son continued the Martin & Martin practice.

THOMAS WALTER FRANCIS NEWTON was educated in Somerset and was then articled to Osborn & Reading of Birmingham. He first practised on his own and then took A. E. Cheatle as his partner. Apart from the City Arcade off Union Street, with its excellent terracotta main frontage in a Flemish Renaissance style, the firm's most important work was done on many business offices and professional chambers on the Colmore estate in Newhall, Edmund, Church, and Cornwall streets. Some of Newton's surviving buildings are neo-Georgian and neo-Jacobean or display simpler Arts and Crafts façades. Some of their details, including railings, gates and lead panelling, are extremely attractive. Newton, who belonged to various cultural and literary organisations, was only forty when he died in 1903. Had he lived he would probably have been one of Birmingham's best early twentieth-century architects.

YEOVILLE THOMASON was born in Edinburgh in 1826, but came of a prominent Birmingham family and was a grandson of Sir Edward Thomason the leading button and toy-maker and Boulton's successor as the chief local manufacturer of coins and medals. Such a connection, and being a pupil of Charles Edge, placed him well for the important civic commissions which came his way. Soon after he had qualified as an architect he managed the architectural department of the borough surveyor's office. He preferred classical architecture to Gothic and admired Wren. He worked on private houses and on a few churches where he was normally obliged to use mid-Victorian Gothic idioms. He designed banks and offices, the lavishly

Renaissance Union Club in Colmore Row, the Aston Workhouse of about 1865, two newspaper offices, and industrial buildings. His best known building, for which he won a competition, is the Council House, dated 1874 and finished in 1878; its extension, with its portico and campanile, is also by Thomason. Among his later works were the Jaffray Hospital, the Chamberlain Arms Hotel appropriately sited in Corporation Street, and Lewis' store which was Birmingham's first iron and concrete building, finished in 1886, the year in which Yeoville Thomason retired from practice. He died in London in 1901.

Thomason is an architect whose work is hard to admire. But its sheer quantity, and the prominence of the Council House, made him an important figure in the city's building history.

WILLIAM HENRY WARD was born in Scotland in 1844, and was articled to James Cranston of Oxford who designed two Gothic Nonconformist churches in Birmingham. Ward came to Birmingham in 1865, and built up a large and varied practice, particularly on public buildings, though hotels, restaurants, and the well known Great Western Arcade were also by him. He designed the late Victorian Gothic block at the Dudley Road Infirmary and the City Sanatorium, and worked on workhouses, sanatoria and hospitals in several towns other than Birmingham; his scope extended to public markets in Mexico City. His restoration jobs included work at Maxstoke and Warwick Castles. He died in 1917.

Acknowledgements

Among many people who have, in various ways, helped me during my work on this book I have to thank Mr F. W. Bradnock, MBE, the City of Birmingham's Public Relations Officer; Mr Neville Borg, MICE, the City Surveyor, Engineer and Planning Officer, and members of his staff; and Mr W. G. Reed, ARIBA and Mr J. C. Harkness, ARIBA of the City Architect's department. Miss D. M. Norris, lately of the Local History Department of the Central Reference Library, Birmingham, and members of the staff there have been of the greatest assistance. I have also to thank Mr R. Temple Cox, ARIBA, the Honorary Secretary of the Birmingham Civic Society; Dr R. J. Hetherington, and Mr Remo Granelli, FRIBA, and Dr Rachel Waterhouse of the Victorian Society; and Mr Francis Greenacre, now of the Bristol Art Gallery. I have had useful assistance from Mr R. G. Lewis, Assistant Bursar, University of Birmingham; Mr Philip Rahtz of the Department of History; Mr T. H. Bowyer, Deputy Librarian and Dr K. W. Humphreys of the Library; and the Rev Dr Gilbert Cope of the Institute for the Study of Worship and Religious Architecture. At the University of Aston, to which the School of Architecture in the College of Art and Design is affiliated, I have had most kind help from Professor Denys Hinton, Mr Oscar Naddermeier and Mr Martin Purdy, and I also owe a debt of gratitude to Mr David Barclay, ARIBA, of the Birmingham Building Centre.

I have to thank the Rev R. G. Lunt, MA, Chief Master of the King Edward VI School; Mr D. B. Gaskin, MA, Headmaster of Moseley Grammar School, and members of his staff; Rev C. L. Mitton, late Principal of Handsworth College; and the Rev C. Buckmaster, BA, and Miss Joan Smith, Librarian, St Peter's College, Saltley. Also Mr C. V. Baker, General Manager of Sutton Dwellings Trust; Miss M. Lygo, Secretary of Harborne Tenants Ltd; Mrs E. Allen, Public Relations Assistant, BSA Co Ltd; Mr R. P. Lee, Proof Master at Birmingham Gun Barrel Proof House; Mr K. F. Wortelhock and Mrs H. S. Blizzard of the Public Relations Office, Mitchells & Butlers Ltd.

At Cadbury's I had most useful help from Mr T. Insull, the editor of the Bournville Works Magazine, and Mr J. M. Murtagh, ARIBA, of the firm's architectural department. Mr Selby Clewer, FRIBA, of the Bournville Village Trust was also most helpful.

Mr E. Grizzell, Public Relations Officer for the John Madin Design Group, helped me with information on the work of that architectural partnership. Among architects I have to thank are Mr Neville Hawkes, FRIBA, of Harry Bloomer & Son; Mr A. E. Chatwin, FRIBA; Mr Kenneth Wood, FRIBA, of the J. Seymour Harris Partnership; Mr Noel Hastilow, ARIBA, of Holland W. Hobbiss & Partners; various staff members of James A. Roberts; Mr A. L. Hall, FRIBA, and Mr L. Palmer Renton, ARIBA, of Harry W. Weedon & Partners; Mr J. Edmundson, ARIBA, of Desmond Williams & Associates, Manchester; Mr Robert Brandt, FRIBA, of Sir Giles Scott, Son & Partners, London; Mr W. G. Howell, FRIBA, of Howell, Killick, Partridge & Amis, London; and Mr Keith Barnes, ARIBA, of Arup Associates, London.

I have also had much kind assistance from the library, and the records section of the RIBA.

B.D.G.L.
Bristol, March 1971

Illustrations

City of Birmingham: Art Gallery, 5, 6; Reference Library (photographs by W. G. Belsher), 9, 10, 13, 16, 17, 19, 20, 21, 24, 38, 39, 40, 43, 46, 48, 49; Information Department, 22, 25, 26, 33, 37, 88, 100; Office of the City Architect, 98, 99; Water Department, 78. Photographs by Dennis Assinder, 1, 2, 3, 4, 7, 15, 27, 28, 31, 36, 41, 50, 57, 64 (by kind permission of A. E. Chatwin, FRIBA), 58, 59, 60, 62, 63, 67, 68 and 70 (by kind permission of the City Engineer and Planning Officer), 71, 72, 73, 74, 75, 89, 90. Photographs by D. Cauldwell, 30, 47, 51, 52, 54, 55, 56, 66, 76, 77, 85, 86, 87.

National Monuments Record, 8, 11, 12, 18, 23, 32, 34, 42, 61, 83; from drawings by the author, 14; Proof Master, Gun Barrel Proof House, 29; Lewis Brown Associates, 35; Chief Master, King Edward VI School, 44; The Procurator, Oscott College, 45; The Superior, The Oratory, 84; BSA Co Ltd, 53; Botteley & Co, 65; Mr Francis Greenacre, 69; Cadbury Bros Ltd, 79; Bournville Village Trust, 80, 81, 104; Mitchells & Butlers Ltd, 91; John Madin Design Group, 92, 95; J. Seymour Harris Partnership, 93, 94; James A. Roberts, ARIBA, jacket, 96, 97; Harry Bloomer & Son, 101; Harry W. Weedon & Partners, 102, 103; Bromilow, While & Smeeton, 105; Desmond Williams & Associates, 106; Sir Giles Scott, Son & Partners, 107, 108; Professor Denys Hinton, FRIBA, 109; Mr Martin Purdy, 110; Howell, Killick, Partridge & Amis, 111; Arup Associates, 112.

Index plate numbers are indicated in bold type